# The Mystery in School Finances

# The Mystery in School Finances

## *Discovering Answers in Community-Based Budgeting*

Matthew Malinowski

Published in cooperation with Association of School Business
Officials, International
ROWMAN & LITTLEFIELD
Lanham • Boulder • New York • Toronto • Plymouth, UK

Published by Rowman & Littlefield
4501 Forbes Boulevard, Suite 200, Lanham, Maryland 20706
www.rowman.com

10 Thornbury Road, Plymouth PL6 7PP, United Kingdom

British Library Cataloguing in Publication Information Available

**Library of Congress Cataloging-in-Publication Data**

Malinowski, Matthew.
The mystery in school finances : discovering answers in community-based budgeting / Matthew Malinowski.
p. cm.
Includes bibliographical references.
ISBN 978-1-4758-0987-9 (cloth : alk. paper) -- ISBN 978-1-4758-0988-6 (pbk. : alk. paper) -- ISBN 978-1-4758-0989-3 (electronic)
1. Education--United States--Finance. 2. School budgets--United States. 3. Community and school--United States. I. Title.
LB2825.M14 2014
379.1'210973--dc23

2014006100

∞™ The paper used in this publication meets the minimum requirements of American National Standard for Information Sciences Permanence of Paper for Printed Library Materials, ANSI/NISO Z39.48-1992.

Printed in the United States of America

A dedication to the MIMA LOMA team!
Together the potential is unlimited.

# Contents

# Acknowledgments

The acknowledgment of the Association of School Business Officials and Pennsylvania Association of School Business Officials, the latter who provided resources to develop a master's in public administration into the ability to positively impact one of the poorest districts in Pennsylvania and now to work with one of the most diverse and committed to education of all children, the school district of Cheltenham Township, and the former for their role in providing a monthly publication from which I was approached by Rowman & Littlefield Publishers, Inc., to expand upon and is successfully completed in the pages contained within.

In addition, an acknowledgment has to be made for Dr. Robert C. Carriker and his wife Eleanor who, when I was trying to figure out what options laid ahead for me, guided me with support, encouragement, and realistic options, which led me down my career path. I have continued to be supported by others along the way, but Bob and Eleanor started me on a path I am pleased I took. Along the path, there have been numerous supporters to note and thank for their ideas, encouragement, and wisdom. In particular, the Montgomery County School Business Officials, the school district of Cheltenham Township Board of Directors (who I would challenge value the role of education in developing the future of all students more than any other political group), former superintendents, office staff, and colleagues.

# Foreword

Let's get one thing perfectly clear right out of the chute: You may be thinking that this is just another book about budgeting, but you are wrong. It's not—it's the real deal! If you are interested in education at any level, then this book is a must-read.

The school district's budget is the proverbial tail that wags the dog. Not a science, but an art, budget development is the school system's road map to success. Over the past thirty-five years, I have seen all types of budgets: the good, the bad, and the ugly. I have seen budgets make the school systems the success they are known for, and I have seen budgets throw school systems into a tail spin. I have seen budgets that created a sense of trust and camaraderie within the community, and I have seen communities wrought with anger and mistrust, diverting the focus from student needs to adult issues that should have never surfaced.

A school district's success depends in large part on the budget document and the stakeholders' involvement in and commitment to it.

Matt Malinowski is a seasoned professional who understands the critical role the budget plays in the success of the school district and the community. When he asked me to write the foreword for this book, I was excited—not because he asked me to write the foreword, but because of the importance of the topic and the long-range ramifications budgeting has on not only the school district, but the community at large. I was excited because like Matt, I recognize the impact the budget has on the children.

I can't think of anyone more qualified to write a book that is based on practical methods and case studies than Matt Malinowski. He is insightful, skilled, and a true professional in school business management. This work reflects his dedication to school business. Matt presents the topics in a comprehensive, thorough, practical way. He offers not only wisdom, but practical

*Foreword*

strategies that are applicable in myriad situations. This book offers a road map to success. It is an easy read, yet insightful, and certainly a reference that school district leaders will keep in their library and reach for time after time.

I urge you to read on with zest and enthusiasm. Just as Matt clearly has done, we should pour our hearts and souls into making the children in our communities the best that they can be.

**–John D. Musso, CAE**
**Executive Director**
**Association of School Business Officials International**

# Preface: What Can You Do?

School districts are arguably one of the biggest expenditures of public funds. The significance of school budgets is they are reliant on state and local revenue sources. While the federal government sets education policies and drives out some funding, the reliance for funds is in the hands of states and local revenues. In difficult economic times and even the best of times, the decisions that school districts make are critical not only to the future generations, but to implications on state and local resources.

By your attraction to this book, it may be concluded that you have a sincere interest in public education and perhaps more specifically in school district budgets. While the logistics of a budget process rests on professionals, as taxpayers and citizens interested in promoting the common good, there are certainly ways to become involved in the public education system. Through individuals working to improve the system, the system will continue to be sustained for years to come.

This book provides a straightforward discussion of practices, which school districts utilize to include communities in the budget process. From the assessment of needs, wants, and desires, to discussions of the budget as a policy document and year-round process, this book provides insight into the methods and process for both professionals in the field and constituents seeking insight into the process. School budgets are not a one-size-fits-all, but a reflection of the community served and a collaboration of a variety of stakeholders.

Through incorporating case studies and practical solutions, this book is a valuable resource for administrators and members of the public at large. Additionally, the book provides a focus on the policy issues and variety of dynamics that relate to fiscal matters. These discussions are not just matters of accounting but provide their own challenges for which there is not a one-size-fits-all solution.

# Introduction

Often, school budgets can be a contentious process. Complicated information that drives both short- and long-term decision-making is discussed. The variety of views on the needs, wants, and desires at times conflict or seem to land to an unclear pathway.

There are critical roles in the budget process for the superintendent, finance officer, and internal and external stakeholders. The superintendent functions similar to a chief executive officer. In his/her role, the superintendent is the main go-to between the board of directors and the district. Providing a vision for the school district as a whole is critical in working to ensure community engagement to provide a comprehensive 360-degree perspective that drives the budget process to ensure it reflects the community served.

School budgets, regardless of geography, follow state procedures for both development and approval. These perfunctory tasks include putting a budget on display for viewing, receipt of public comment, and a vote. What this book seeks to provide are ideas for incorporating ongoing community discussion and dialogue on the budget process. Additionally, this book will provide insight and information into the budget process that drives all school decisions.

As a starting point of information, I am providing here a "top-ten" of the must knows regarding the school budget process.

*10. Budgets include factors from prior, current, and future fiscal years.*

The budget discussion for an upcoming year is not the only consideration. Past decisions relative to tax increases or expenditure reductions can impact the actions during budget development. Additionally, future impacts such as debt service, enrollment, and facilities needs also have a substantial impact on what must occur within the budget. An examination of multiple prior and future years in addition to the current year is essential to develop a representative budget that considers short- and long-term impacts.

## 9. Budgets can ordinarily be modified within a school year.

The planning and exactitude that goes into preparing school budgets is a well-known fact; however, the "business of education" is fluid. Ordinarily, school districts review baseline expenditures once the school year is up and running to determine what adjustments need to be made. Additionally, the length of time between certain expenditure and revenue estimates and final prior year expenditures can impact the current year budget. It is the responsibility of a school district to adjust and respond to budget uncertainties as well as seek to provide for changes in the educational program.

## 8. Budget uncertainty is a significant factor for why schools cannot operate on a budget cycle similar to the corporate world.

Perhaps one of the more unique factors for school budgets is the inability to reduce services due to federal and state requirements. For example, if an outside placement for a student was not budgeted, the placement cannot simply be denied. Additionally, as school budgets are comprised of significant personnel and benefit costs, those can fluctuate based upon benefit elections, leaves of absence, and other factors such as required individual student support and staff to fulfill class size expectations.

To reduce the uncertainty, districts often include a budgetary reserve to fund unanticipated costs; however, gauging what uncertain costs will be is a problem, which can lead to a surplus or deficit if the reserve is not adequate. Looking at history as well as constant review of revenues and expenditures are ways a district can implement best practices to ensure it is meeting budgetary goals and delivering appropriate educational programs for all students.

## 7. Budgets provide an allocation that dictates goals and initiatives.

Unfortunately, there is not a finite amount of revenues. Additionally, due to tolerance for increased local revenues or lack of state and federal funding, there is a reality that funds need to be allocated. In part, this fact determines what funding will drive specific annual initiatives. There is a correlation to the fact that something may or may not be in a budget and what will take place around that area for goals, objectives, and results in the budget year. Finally, while a district may seek to disburse funds in small amounts for a variety of initiatives, the lack of full support it takes to complete a goal or objective can reduce the results and cost benefit of the expenditure allocation.

*6. Budgets can be impacted by factors not associated with the district's operation.*

At its simplest form, a budget is about balancing expenditures and revenues. If only it were that simple. There are numerous factors to account for that are not necessarily under control or the decision-making authority of a school district. On the revenue side, these can include political pressures, inclination to tax increases, changes in state funding distributions, and economic factors such as interest and tax revenue generation.

For expenditures, costs for out of district placements, mandates to transportation, and even the more recent federal mandate for affordable healthcare are examples of drivers that a school district has no say in the costs but can adjust variables and mitigate the overall impact through modifications to programs. Additionally, natural disasters and other factors regarding maintaining viable programs can be curveballs to an intended budget plan. While the demands may be inflexible, the role of the chief financial officer is to prepare the roadmap to navigate the district through unexpected variables.

*5. Budgets have ups and downs.*

Budgets begin as best laid plans but rarely are passed in a final form, which represents the initial proposal. That fact is a good thing. Budgets must reflect the community values as well as the most current fiscal situation. Additionally, as previously mentioned, the fiscal situation can change and budgets should not reflect only an initial conception, but rather a responsive document. Finally, due to the nature of community input and discussions, issues can come up that are hot and outside issues can be linked to the budget complicating the process.

*4. Budget presentations can make or break understanding of issues and factors.*

Presentations are key to providing a foundation for understanding. Providing a contextual understanding of numbers and trends is essential to ensuring the correct message and overtone is delivered. Perhaps more an art than science, budget presentations should provide factual and complete information that is not too detailed or too summative. Truly great budget presentations anticipate the needs, wants, and desires of the group to which they are presented.

*3. Budgets must reflect reality.*

In order to provide a guiding blueprint for current and future endeavors, budgets must be accurate and appropriately allocate funds to actual costs. A budget that negates certain costs or which inflates revenues will not only fail as a policy document, but misrepresent the financial picture. In addition to representing accurate revenues and expenditures, budgets have to include what can reasonably be estimated to occur. For example, if enrollment will increase, appropriate staff should be included to comply with board policy or guidelines. Finally, budgets should reflect those programs and initiatives that will be acted on, not just talked about or part of a filed strategic plan.

## 2. Budgets are political.

Budgets include numbers, but as previously stated provide a policy and programmatic framework for the school entity. Additionally, the fact that budgets can be approached from a variety of perspectives and viewpoints can prove challenging. Despite the best intent to develop cohesive and representative goals, school budgets can turn debatable. In these times, the role of the administration is to fulfill the factual role of providing information requested and working within the parameters established by the board of directors.

## 1. Budget development is not one-size-fits-all.

There are a multitude of models and best practices on budget development as no school district is the same. The best budget development occurs when the school district is versed and benchmarked in budget development practices and incorporates local decision-making and practice into the budget process. Benchmarking the school district to similar demographic, geographic, and other factors is perhaps the best way to ensure budgeting is appropriate and progressive.

   The key to budget development is linking the budget to educational goals and objectives. Additionally, multi-year strategic budgeting looks at past, present, and future revenues and expenditures to support the district's educational endeavors. Incorporating opportunities for stakeholder feedback along the road to developing a final budget is essential and hopefully you will find this book useful in generating ideas and stimulating solutions to what you wish to improve in your school budget process.

*Chapter One*

# Community-based Budgeting

Implementation of community-based budgeting is of the utmost importance in this day and time. Unprecedented economic situations have forced school districts to do more with less. Unlike other sectors, school districts have to meet a variety of needs, of which many are mandated.

The needs of school districts include those both for mandated educational programs such as special education and other instructional programs as well as the often overlooked mandated needs such as facilities, transportation, and other services. With the current economic constraints facing our country, school districts have been pushed to develop annual budgets through a new lens and accept the reality that budget adoption is a complex and political process.

Whether a school district is rich or poor, growing or declining in enrollment, serving a specialized population, or relying primarily on state or local revenue, there seems to be general public dissatisfaction with the school district budget process. This book aims at providing possibilities for a different path to the final budget adoption.

Of utmost importance was what Stephen Covey in his book *The 7 Habits of Highly Effective People* labeled "Habit 2: Begin with the End in Mind." For the school district of Cheltenham Township, the "end" was to develop a budget that supported a school system according to the district motto: where excellence begins with education and values the unique programs in the academics, arts, and athletics. The "end" also needed to be accomplished through community collaboration.

It is important that a school district reflects the community for which it stands to serve. The school district is built upon the desires, expectations, and ultimately financial resources of the community it serves. Regardless of

1

whether the school is funded by local, state, or federal revenues, the funds under which it operates, public funds, are at stake.

## HOW DO BUDGETS IMPACT PROGRAMS?

School districts are program driven. Without programs, there would be no schools. Moreover, school districts are often defined and referred to by the programs they offer. Good, strong programs attract parents who want to provide their children with such opportunities. For example, offering significant arts and music programs can attract parents. A high number of advanced placement programs speak to the academic rigor of the high school programs and the opportunities for students to be exposed to a college curriculum.

Out of this root connection, school budgets are the most important non-instructional decision a district reviews. While the budget itself is a financial exercise, it directly impacts what curriculum and other decisions the district will make. Therefore, the basis of a decision for whether taxes are raised or expenditure drivers reduced means a direct impact to program.

The idea of a seesaw seems to maintain a balance between fiscal prudence and opportunities for developing children. Schools must meet not only the needs of the general population but also the needs of children with special or gifted needs as well as those with an inclination to vocational and other programs. An extreme reliance on financial factors to drive programs can adversely impact programs while conversely, program-driven budgets that fail to account for an economic reality probably do not provide long-term stability.

The balance on the financial piece in part seems to ensure program efficiency and meet student needs through a variety of opportunities that serve all students. Finding the balance is one-sided if an administration and school board are the only priorities involved. Community-based budgeting begins with considering the constituent base. Uncovering the values represented and working through the budget process with clear and consistent communication results in greater understanding in not only the budget, but the organization's values.

Community-based budgeting, therefore, requires a community that seeks to promote programs to serve the needs of all students and respond to a changing environment. For most school districts, this is dictated by federal and state mandates as well as by salary and benefit costs.

This book will address critical components of community-based budgeting and explain how the budget process can easily work in an environment in which the board, administration, faculty, and residents want to create excellent educational opportunities in a fiscally responsible fashion.

## COMPONENTS THAT CREATE SCHOOL BUDGETS

Muddying the waters one more level is the fact that school programs are driven by the cost to employ people. Personnel costs for any school district are the largest percent of a budget. Budget information should be easily available to the public, yet the numbers prove to be highly emotional; there is a tendency to make assumptions and to rally around certain personnel or programmatic decisions. Often, personnel will spawn this dissent and will seek to protect their territory and role.

Regardless of whether the personnel is an aide, professional staff, or administrator, there will be segments of the community for and against decisions that dictate personnel and which ultimately impact programs. While there is no remedy to this process, there is a need for the administration and school board to be a focus on the overall driver of the district budget. The most common driver of programs provided by a school is personnel.

Salaries and benefits are a component of program costs. Just like a program cannot exist without books, supplies, or technology, it cannot exist without people. Administrators factor in at a small percentage of overall costs. Salaries and benefits as a percentage of the budget directed to the administration should be benchmarked to retain decision-making authority for what, beyond an established standard, is required to deliver programs and to serve the community.

In addition to the salary and benefit costs, the next largest expenditures are mandated programs costs such as student placements and needs to meet federal and state requirements. This includes performance targets coupled with the costs for operating functional and safe facilities and systems of transportation.

Facilities costs include not only personnel such as previously mentioned, but maintenance, compliance with safety code requirements, and responding to natural causes and incidents beyond a district's control. Augmenting facilities costs for many districts is the fact that schools function as an organization that serves the community at large and very often outside of the school day. Numerous government, civic, and other outside organizations utilize school buildings. These entities do not have resources to pay for actual usage costs that would factor in utilities and other overhead such as cleaning, staff, etc., being attributed to facilities maintenance costs.

Additionally, facility costs are very often substantially more than can be accommodated in a general fund budget. Long-term debt service (similar to a loan) is taken out to repay for the major project over a period of time (twenty to thirty years on average). Debt service is ordinarily upwards of 10 percent of a district's overall budget and is a positive sign that there is a commitment to facilities. While there can be varying levels of debt, debt service that is too low may indicate that improvements are not being made, while high debt may indicate that too much is being financed over a long-term, which will increase the district's extended obligations and bind future financial resources.

Transportation expenditures are to transport students to and from schools and other school-based activities. Busing is often a large expenditure that varies by the topography and distribution of the community. Paired with the need for safety as a paramount concern, transportation's impact on a budget can increase or decrease due to demand.

In addition, there is the need in every school for transportation to serve all students. All students means that regardless of location, physical limitation, or other obstacles, students need to be transported. Later in the book, we will discuss "wants" of a community. "Wants" translate to expectations of the community, in particular transportation costs due to the "wants" of a community relative to service levels and other conveniences that redirect resources away from student instructional programs.

This is not to belittle the remaining areas of school expenditures, which include supplies, equipment, and other costs, but to make the point that important expenditures of these types are ordinarily a small percentage of the overall expenditures. Districts have some say in these expenditures, but to an extent items such as paper, copiers, ink, and pens are necessary for the district to function. Reductions in these areas with no plan or thought can dramatically impact the program and operational function of the school district.

Additionally, there is also a community perception with students not having enough basic resources. School districts in response to economic hardships have made headlines for asking students to bring in their own supplies and even items such as paper towels, tissues, and toilet paper. However, this argument does not logically translate to saying that a school district needs to buy whatever the students desire or want. It is the responsibility of the school district to provide those components that impact instruction to include both those items directly in a classroom and those which are part of the overall district climate.

## COMMUNITIES HAVE A VESTED INTEREST

Based upon the composition of what makes up a school budget and the weight of importance in delivering a strong educational program at a reasonable cost, communities must be well informed about their budget. While the board ultimately enacts a budget, the community needs to understand what action is being taken regardless of the economic situation.

The role of budgets in a community establishes a framework for the initiatives and other objectives of the school year for that time period. Budgets from year to year are building blocks to the evolution of the district. The programs, services, and meeting goals, objectives, and targets are the building blocks to school budgets. When a budget provides resources in a planned and targeted fashion, measureable objectives are met and the education for students is improved.

Ordinarily, citizen interest in a school budget peaks when taxes are being raised or program cuts are proposed. The interest is purely from an individual or from those impacted adversely by the action. This should not be the case, but in many districts across the United States it seems to be the norm. Community budgeting encourages citizen involvement and feedback but as a representative for all students, not a certain subset or to stand strong to protect singular or non-global interests.

Members of the community from those who are engaged to those who are disengaged should seek to be informed about the school budget. The budget development process must allow for input. Reasonable concerns provide an important part of the budget process. Community-based budgeting involves citizens receiving information about a budget that will drive school programs and desired outcomes.

## COMMUNITIES CAN MAKE A DIFFERENCE

Rather than simply dissenting to actions, the more informed a community is, the more that community can either change behavior or make constructive recommendations relative to the steps being taken. Becoming informed means not only utilizing information provided on finances, but also on programs, benchmark data, best practices, and research studies from reputable sources.

For example, perhaps in adverse economic times a new school should not be built. Perhaps in better times, money should be saved for a long-term need. All decisions have consequences and can strengthen or weaken the district and provide an opportunity or direct future actions. One of the cornerstones of making sound decisions for educational programs is the budget and financial components of revenues, expenditures, and a term defined later called fund balance.

Rational and informed community members can endeavor to support the board and administration in their decisions. Informed community members can advocate to outside groups such as state legislators to maintain funding or direct money to where it can best serve students, which is the reason schools exist. There is the potential for significant legislative influence if each and every parent advocated to either legislators or to community-based groups about the value of schools and the constant dwindling resources directed to schools in light of the burdens and accountability they bear.

A closing thought to build on the need for both those vested and non-vested in a school district that they reside in is to recognize the moving target of increasing expectations from parents, state boards, and the federal government. Additionally, there is a lack of realization that to a "reasonable" extent, funding does not match the expectations. A saying that relays this best is the realization that US defense obtains significant resources and funding and yet education falls to "bake sales" to meet funding needs. When will the day come when the Air Force will have to hold a bake sale to purchase bombs?

## WHAT WOULD YOU DO?

Perhaps nothing demonstrates the critical dynamics of a process more than "real world scenarios." Any administrator or school board member could provide an ample deck of scenarios relative to a topic; however, scenarios are only as valuable a resource as the lens from which we examine them and understand the perspective that each person involved brings to the table.

For the sake of the examples in this book, all are real scenarios; however, specifics have been retracted so as to not directly relay an organization or individuals. Additionally, when reading the case studies, it is important to look at the various perspectives that directly relate to those identified in Chapter 1.

The first case study reveals the competing interests that each perspective brings. Once you read the scenario, consider what you would do or think you would do to work through the situation. As you continue to read through the book, ponder the issues the case raised, which will be joined together in a concluding chapter.

## CASE STUDY: SUCCESSFUL COMMUNITY-BASED BUDGETING

In light of seeking to reduce expenditures while maximizing efficiency and effectiveness in operations, school districts have developed community task forces. These initiatives draw experts and the general population of a community to review revenue, expenditures, and other matters relating to costs from a policy level. They can be successful, and they can be a process that does not produce productive and tangible results.

There are many best practices for these task forces. Districts from around the nation have turned to them recognizing the impact of declining revenues and increasing costs of providing an educational program. The success of such an initiative is dependent on the perspective brought to the table by the community and the administration.

Regardless of the financial deficit, the programs in play, or the final outcome, and the mindset matter most. The mindset must be that there are confines that have to be worked within and challenges from different lenses. Ultimately, a decision must be made in the best interest of the district aligned to best practices and initiatives in the community with an understanding that there must be an outcome regardless of how undesirable either option may be.

Two districts developed budget workgroups drawing those who volunteered from the community. No community member was turned away, and everyone was able to participate. Meetings took place and reviewed expenditures, revenues, trends, and policies on educational and operational objectives. Additionally, there were notes taken and appropriate follow-up made in the process.

Recommendations from both groups were incorporated into the districts plans for spending. Targets and a timeline for implementation were developed. Administrators were prepared to take necessary steps to ensure fiscal stability.

In the following year, the first district found itself in a position to have one of the highest state-wide tax increases. Despite the work and recommendations, there was still a significant gap between revenues and expenditures. The other district prepared a balanced budget with no tax increase for the second year in a row. However, in seeking to be forward thinking, the district presented a follow-up to the public on more specific steps to implement ideas generated at the task force.

In the district that sought to present subsequent follow-up ideas, the community approached the ideas adversely. There was scrutiny of certain initiatives and ideas. The main interest was in what reductions would be made in the foreseeable future and how their children would be impacted. After this meeting, the school district provided a summary of objectives and continued to work for reductions through the course of the next year.

- What involvement could the district with the tax increase in year two have with the community in the second year?
- What message was sent by the community members at the other district in the second year?
- At this point, what parallels do you see between the two districts?
- Can you anticipate any issues that may be present?
- What role has the administration and community played the financial success of each district? What role do you anticipate them playing in the financial success of each district?

*Chapter Two*

# Historical School Budgets

Historically, school budgets follow a process based on step-by-step procedures. Budgets are developed by the administration and presented to the governing board and public. Budgets must be balanced with accurate estimates of revenues and expenditures.

Development of a budget requires detailed plans for the programs and services a school district will operate for the coming fiscal year. An estimate of the resources necessary to accomplish the goals of each program and service is also needed. Once the resources are identified, the costs, which include staffing, facilities, and other expenditures, must be determined. At the same time, the revenue that will be used to support the district's operations must be estimated and expenditure plans adjusted to meet available funding plans.[1]

Throughout the course of the process, budget feedback is received usually through a hearing from members of the public at large. While certainly a viable process, it often pits members of the community against the board and administration. It sets up an adversarial environment that is not the most constructive or productive use of time.

Additionally, it becomes challenging to have a productive meeting as public comments are received, analyzed outside of the formal meeting, and then reported back at the next meeting. The ability for the district to demonstrate the working process is minimized. Concurrently, the ability for substantive dialogue with members of the community is diminished due to the adversarial nature.

The traditional communication and feedback process for budget development has and continues to be utilized in schools time and time again. Community-based budgeting suggests that there is an alternative approach as part of the traditional process that can be instituted to not only provide a better

9

end product, but also to improve information flow. Information flow is both to and from the community on the schools strategic plan, capital initiatives, and other long-term areas of focus.

## BUDGET PROCESS

There is a sequence of events and milestones that must be met to comply with legal requirements at the state and local level. A sample budget calendar is provided in Table 2.1.

The first part of the budget process is the development of numerous documents to delineate for internal stakeholders the process and procedures for submission. Often outlined in a procedure manual, the framework is set for the development of the budget. Additionally, this document indicates any goals to be met or actions to be taken by site-based administrators in the development of the budget.

Concurrently with the development and distribution of a budget manual, a budget timeline is developed. The timeline explains milestones and high-lights in the process as far as deadlines for submission, meeting dates, and other important filing or compliance deadlines. The timeline is a critical component to the process. Without it there is no accountability relative to budget development.

The next step is an examination of enrollment trends to determine the enrollment that the school district will serve next year. Enrollment drives many of the largest cost factors for school districts, including personnel and facilities. Enrollment trends dictate whether additional staff or facility mod-ifications will be necessary for inclusion in the budget.

Developing enrollment data includes migrating students to the next grade level and including live births and other demographic shifts. Accurate enroll-ment projections ensure resources such as professional and support staff is available to meet needs and achieve desired outcomes.

Additionally, revenues are impacted by enrollment. Very often subsidies and other funds are distributed based upon enrollment numbers. Revenue projections as a whole are developed well before expenditure projections. Similar to a salary you may earn which drives your spending, revenues establish a basis for how a school district can spend funds.

Unfortunately, not only economics but also adversity to tax increases has led school budgets to be developed based upon the projected revenues. It may seem odd, but it is practical. When expenditures exceed revenues, as they often do, actions including revenue augmentation are then reviewed.

If a budget cannot include additional revenues, the focus is then on the ability to use reserves or to reduce expenditures. Ideally, it is more logical to determine the spending plan and then calculate revenue needs. What prevents

**Table 2.1. Example of Budget Development Timetable with Benchmark Dates**

| Task and Assignment | Internal Timetable | External Timetable |
|---|---|---|
| 1. Business office completes year-end closing and determines "prior year" actual. | August | — |
| 2. Business office completes current year projected actual. | September | — |
| 3. Business office applies preliminary assumptions to projected actual expenditures and determines the "cost to duplicate" the current year's program at next year's rates; business office prepares preliminary revenue budget. | October | — |
| 4. Administration reviews budget estimates and develops recommendations for increases in discretionary accounts; administration reviews strategic plan and determines financial effect on new budget year. | October | — |
| 5. Administration distributes site-based budget packets; site managers begin working on detailed budget. | October | — |
| 6. Administration continues to review external changes and their effect on the budget; site managers continue to work on budget detail. | January | March |
| 7. Sites return completed budget modules to the business office. | March | — |
| 8. Business office assembles detailed budget document. | April | — |
| 9. Administration continues to review external changes and their effect on the budget; site managers continue to work on budget detail. | April | April |
| 10. Administration presents revised and detailed proposed budget to the board; board accepts, rejects, or modifies; board authorizes administration to prepare final budget document and advertise intention to adopt a final budget. | — | May |
| 11. Administration continues to review external changes and their effect on the final budget document; board adopts final budget; board sets tax levy. | May–June | June |

this is an adversity to tax increases driven by what could be perceived as unlimited expenditure cost increases.

Once a revenue budget is developed, the mandated expenditures are examined including personnel, benefits, state mandates, and debt. Usually nearly 90 percent of a budget is mandated through a variety of policies or regulations at the federal, state, and local level. The budget assumes contractual needs are met for staffing and a status quo or program expansion is aligned with other district goals and objectives.

The fact that revenue generation becomes a hurdle for maintaining "ideal" expenditure levels is in conflict with developing a budget to meet "ideal" goals and objectives. Hence, we fall back to a balance. The seesaw analogy in Chapter 1 comes to the forefront and reminds us that the annual budget strives to maintain balance between the program needs, wants, and desires and the economic reality.

Lastly, discretionary expenditures are culled. Items such as paper, supplies, replacement equipment, and extra pay or overtime are identified. In having discretion over spending, there is an ability to control costs to some extent though not completely. For example, ultimately there has to be traditional school supplies. While they may be scaled back, they must exist to complete the district's core functions.

The framework described previously provides a broad review of the budget process. What is missing is the community. There are in most cases opportunities for public comment but not involvement. Board members who may be elected or appointed are often involved but bear a tremendous obstacle in communicating to constituents the budget reality. The constant involvement of the community in the budget enables a better understanding.

The involvement of the public should not just be limited to the time when the final budget is discussed. The involvement needs to be throughout the budget process and in fact well before the budget for the next year even begins. Strategic plans, five-year plans, committee meetings across all sectors of the community, and operations of the school serve as venues for information.

We began our discussion about the budget as an influential document resulting from an intense process. The budget therefore needs to be an integral part of every step taken by the school district. Involving the community at various intervals and integrating the budget into the program will improve the public's understanding.

Community involvement in outside processes alone does not constitute community-based budgeting. When working on the budget, there needs to be specific, coordinated efforts for involvement. Outside of the budget effort, a rapport must be established with key stakeholders for 360-degree feedback.

## DO SCHOOL BUDGETS REFLECT CORPORATE BUDGETS?

School districts follow a different budgeting process than what is utilized in corporate or personal finance. In the private sector, the budget focuses on profits driven by the income from sales. In public budgeting, the opposite takes place. The theory is that the organization will define its needs, the business function will calculate the costs, and the tax base will supply the funding.[2]

With a changing economy in more recent times, school budgets had reflected this general theory, but have driven to be revenue focused. Revenues drive the ability to determine based on priorities what services the district is able to provide. When there are not substantive revenues to support the expenditures, decisions must be made.

Similar to other public entities such as cities, counties, or municipalities, the focus for school budget is not profit, but stewardship. Dissimilar in nature from the private sector where organizations track finances to record revenues that exceed expenditures, in school budgets the budget shows that the money was spent. The final budget expenditures note how funds were spent in accordance with the goals and objectives outlined during the budget process.

## TRANSITIONING TO MODERN DAY INVOLVEMENT

Traditional budgeting often includes a formal period for the public to review a paper copy. There should also be the opportunity for a public meeting for comments on the budget. Although legislative requirements may remain unchanged and not updated to include more modern opportunities for feedback such as web, chat, and Twitter, there is a substantial opportunity for a school to reach and augment community involvement in the budgeting process through the utilization of such media outlets.

While perhaps useful to gauge a small segment of your community through the traditional budget hearing, to the average citizen, these coordinated events are often either unknown or conflict with schedules. There is value in these face-to-face encounters. However, more often than not, those with either a cause or who are always active in the process are more often in attendance.

With the development of free and widely utilized accessible web and Internet tools, there is the ability to go above mere legal requirements and to reach a wider audience. For example, utilizing Twitter to post and exchange information is a way for the community to integrate updates into their ordinary channels.

Additionally, depending on the community's and district's capabilities, there can be web events and online sessions to review a presentation and provide feedback. These events have the ability to record the session so that those unable to attend are able to review the presentation at a later date and time.

While the Internet can be a viable method to transmit budget information and reach a wider audience, it may not represent the entire composition of the community served. Based upon the fact that school budgets and programs are intricately linked, as many venues as possible should be set up for information exchange such as publications and discussions with individuals and groups. Furthermore, community relationships should be explored and utilized rather than just providing information online. Relationships are developed parallel to the budget process through the interaction of the board and administration with groups such as rotary, churches, and other civic and business groups.

For example, community groups are often beneficial to open dialogue with schools. Whether the composition of the group is retirees, non-profit entities, businesses, or residential associations, the ability to connect in a familiar setting at various intervals throughout the year with these groups proves a worthwhile benefit. Interactions need not be on the budget, but on overall promotion of school activities, goals, and objections. This groundwork provides the ability that in times of fiscal challenges or when critical decisions must be made to either continue credibility or to solicit feedback from these ongoing relationships.

## NON-PUBLIC SCHOOL BUDGETS

For the sake of providing clarity on all school budgets, non-public school budgets differ significantly from public schools. Drawing on sources of revenue such as tuition, and expenditures driven by known and controllable enrollments, the budget is not as volatile from both a production and a vested interest standpoint.

As non-public schools serve individuals who select to attend, there is a similar mindset and goal in those who enroll in the school. Arguably, budget development takes on a different role in part because of this fact.

Additionally, because of the reliance on significantly less (if any) public funds, non-public budgets tend to draw less attention and dispute. It would appear, however, that much of the same "traditional" processes as described previously would be fitting for such an environment with perhaps certain stakeholder feedback. However, this is at a more exacting perspective rather than being diverse and multifaceted.

## CASE STUDY: HISTORIC SCHOOL BUDGETS

Early in my career, I had the fortune of organizing old financial documents for a small school district. As a person who has virtually grown up in a digital age, the task, while seemingly boring and mundane, was eye opening upon further reflection.

Budgets were prepared on greenbar paper or other forms of ledgers. Nearly entirely numerical, they would note expenditures from budgets that barely hit seven figures for an entire school district. The documents were primarily numerical in presentation rarely utilizing charts, graphs, or other manners of visual organization.

There were no enclosed PowerPoints or visually recorded presentations. For some schools, a newsletter and local newspaper captured the essence of the budget by recording increasing expenditures or decreasing revenues.

I could go on about the details of the budget, but it is fair to state that the focus clearly was on numbers. It was accounting and financial management at its best. These documents were effective but only when seeking to provide information from a fiscal perspective.

Current best practices for school budget presentations provide visual stimulation and the ability for pertinent information to be relatively convenient and easier to understand.

- In such an environment where information is always available, is the understanding of school budgets improved?
- Is the budget more understandable than it was when there were simply numbers and narrative?
- Have we gone overboard in the process?
- Consider at this point the knowledge you have of the school district where you live and its budget. Have you easily come across information and other updates?
- Is it all about numbers, or is there are link between program and financial needs?

## NOTES

1. Wood, R. Craig. *School District Budgeting. Principles of School Business Management.* Reston, VA: Association of School Business Officials International, 1986. 12. Print.
2. Keagy, Dale R., and Piper, David M. *Pennsylvania School Business: A Guide for Educational Administrators.* Harrisburg, PA: Pennsylvania Association of School Business Officials 2008. 27. Print.

## Chapter Three

# Balancing Needs, Wants, and Desires

Similar to how we often relate to our personal needs, wants, and desires, school districts have this same thought process relative to their goals and objectives. For example, each day of operation, a school district seeks to maintain a clear focus on what can be done within the budget limitations and community expectations. Building a new middle school may be a desire, but a need is to repair a leaking roof.

There are modicums of forces that drive, delay, and produce the budget, which at its heart is not only a spending plan but also a policy document. A budget establishes not only a short- but long-term action plan and direction for the school district. If something is not included in the budget, there is no ability to fund that initiative.

NEEDS

There is a need to have an appropriate educational program for each and every student. Nearly every district mirrors this need, and it is reflected in the various services funds. These service funds include regular and special instruction, vocational programs, post-twelfth grade enrollment opportunities, support services, capital improvement, and community services. The need is always great and regardless of the district's financial stability outweighs the support necessary to meet the needs.

Administrators often find themselves in an ebb and flow of decision-making. What do I do here, what can we alleviate to meet an unexpected need, etc. Working within a fixed budget is no easy task. Due to the nature of the function that schools serve, there is not a controllable situation in certain cases. For example, a manufacturing company may need to fill a revenue shortfall with reducing expenditures such as labor costs. Schools, however, are different and have an absolute need to provide mandated services.

The needs of a school go back to reflecting the community composition, which is constantly evolving. A myriad of external factors, including economic, social, natural, and other causes, have an impact on student needs, which in turn defines the programmatic needs.

## WANTS

Unlike a need, a want is a short-term notion, which is reflective of a next step. For example, in a budget cycle, the superintendent may want to include new technology in the budget. A principal may want to add an interactive program. While it may supplement a need, it is often a "fist-stab" attempt at meeting a need and not necessarily the most cost-effective step that can be taken.

Unprecedented economic times have focused schools to re-think wants. For example, in wanting to add a mobile computer cart, the level of technology has to be considered. What need will the technology serve? If the need for the technology is just basic programs, the technology need not be as powerful and will subsequently be less expensive.

## FOCUS

There is a fine line between wants and desires. As we make this transition, it is important to stress the need for a focus to meet educational objectives with a limited budget. For example, the budget, as a central policymaking document is critical to focusing administrators, board members, and the community at large. Additionally, the budget lends a focus on the capabilities of the organization as a whole. What can and will be done is reflected in this document.

How does the budget provide this focus? Let's say that a school district would like to add a classroom for exceptional students. The decision to return a program in house can be a significant move for those students who become mainstreamed into the regular instructional program. What if this move has budget implications as far as cost? What needs to be considered?

In the example referenced previously, the administrators look to the budget, which in most districts is approved and developed with community input to provide appropriate direction. If there are no funds available, administrators find themselves balancing the anticipated spending plan with the necessary spending plan. Based upon the appropriate direction that needs to be taken, the budget will be adapted with publically approved budget adjustments or transfers in most cases.

Hence, the budget provides a focus for guiding the educational program. Without it, decisions may be made without proper evaluation or perspective. Focusing on meeting the needs of all students is paramount in an institution with a mission related to educating students in kindergarten through grade twelve.

## DESIRES

Desires can be both those envious situations such as a state-of-the-art high school and higher, less tangible notions such as a desire to have every student reach a top academic performance measure. Both tangible and altruistic desires take funds and drive a budget in their achievement. Recommendations of skilled administrators with degrees and hands on experience influence the community to easily recognize the desires.

The difficulty is in prioritizing and focusing on desires for which funding can be obtained. Even though a desire has merit, the ability to implement it rests on the capacity of a school district's budget. In tight budget times, the ability to implement then rests on the creativity of the responsible administrator in examining how to change status quo to provide resources.

Desires must be associated with balance. Similar to those that a child may have, there is the potential for desires to be "off the beaten path." For example, there is the need to maintain a focus in the desires brought forth from the community in an organization. Prioritization, which will be discussed later in this book, is an example of focusing desires.

The desire of a community to meet the needs of a highly over-identified student program may come from the community to the administration and be evaluated and determined to not be of appropriate merit. In this case, it is important that the administration communicate to the community that the proposed delivery of services does not meet the needs of all students. Furthermore, the school continues to strive to appropriately meet the needs for all students through a variety of opportunities.

## VARIOUS APPROACHES TO "MODERN" DAY BUDGETING

Community-based budgeting is unlike other budget methods in that it incorporates systematic feedback into the budget process. Components of budgeting are part of every process and feedback. Dialogue is also integrated into the district processes. While many other "budget trends" include line item, program budgeting, and zero-based budgeting, community-based budgeting incorporates the best practices and allows the idiosyncrasies and needs of an individual district while providing a framework for development.

These popular budget concepts are summarized subsequently. A district's philosophy, goals, and management may choose one or a combination of these characteristics in budget development. Being familiar with each concept may help to understand not only the approach the district has towards budget development but also how the numbers presented are developed and refined.

**Table 3.1.   Popular Budgeting Concepts in the Public School Culture**

| Concept | Characteristic | Advantages | Disadvantages |
|---|---|---|---|
| Performance Based Budgeting | Budget development follows goals, objectives and strategies | Logically follows the strategic plan and organizational direction Focus is in service cost not on the benefits | Intricate process which requires all parties to work in synch |
| Zero Based Budgeting | Assumes that each operating department must justify its existence for each budget cycle | Forces creative and critical thought Appeals to public | Time consuming |
| Level of Service | Assumes that the current level of service is appropriate and duplicates it with an upward cost adjustment | Ease of preparation Easily Understood Focuses energy on new services and improvement | Perpetuates additive nature of government expenditures and services |
| Allocation/Site Based | Assigns pre-determined amounts for budget preparation and control to building principals and other managers; amounts are based on indices or other parameters | Creates Accountability Places analytical work where it is best understood Supports side-based management concepts | Could be counter-productive if superintendent or school board apply centralized control |

Keagy, Dale R. and Piper, David M. Pennsylvania School Business: A Guide for Educational Administrators.(Harrisburg, PA): Pennsylvania Association of School Business Officials 2008.

## PERFORMANCE-BASED BUDGETING

Performance-based budgeting is a process in which there is a focus on the cost of a specific service. Discussions at budget time do not necessarily delve into the policy implications, but rather are directed to the services provided and what the outcome is based upon.

For a school district, performance-based budgeting provides the funding for goals, strategies, and performance measures. The service presented in the budget (e.g., gifted education) would narrate the priorities, outcomes, and effectiveness of the district's gifted program. Rather than merely pining for the resource limitations or allocations, the budget shares outcomes and prioritizations for the program in a highly transparent communication to constituents.

## ZERO-BASED BUDGETING

Zero-based budgeting begins each year's budgeting process with no assumptions that the previous year's allocations will be granted. In this form of budgeting, the budget is built upon what would be needed to accomplish objectives in the next year. For example, staffing is subject to needs, not an entitlement from year to year.

While this sounds like a plausible theory of budgeting, the challenge is the time-consuming nature of this process, which is not where time and energy can be focused when from year to year schools are stable in enrollment and needs. This means that an evaluation of service levels and needs should be done. The analysis of true needs based upon enrollments and other initiatives to improve achievement can be valuable and beneficial if performed annually, but they need not be done for all budget categories.

## LEVEL OF SERVICE

Developing budgets in a level of service environment assumes that from year to year services will be consistent. The budget is built from a status quo mindset. Constructing a budget is relatively straightforward and predictable with consistency from year to year with a calculation of cost increases. Where the level of service budget fails is in the ability to control costs.

An example demonstrates the lack of expenditure control with the level service budget development process. With the advent of technology, secretary roles have moved away from many clerical tasks such as filing, typing, and scheduling. Under the level of service approach, staffing requirements are never considered as far as workload or improved ease in job completion. The level of staffing in this model remains the same from year to year or could increase to maintain a service.

When a service is not considered in light of how to be more efficient and effective, there may be a perception or in fact a reality that fiscal prudence of tax funds is not present. Additionally, as the landscape of education continues to change, services may change and no longer be required or modified to provide a different outcome. Level of service budgeting, while an option, is not necessarily common.

## ALLOCATION/SITE-BASED BUDGETING

Site-based budgeting provides the opportunity for staff such as principals and administrators to have a say in the development of their budget. Budget administrators are charged with developing each and every expenditure they will need to function as a site. For example, requiring additional learning support is a function of the principal, and the mechanics of prioritizing needs, wants, and desires rests with the budget administrator.

Site-based budgeting is an inclusive, cooperative process where budget limitations are communicated and priorities are set by those on the front line. Allocations are given to each budget administrator. As budgets are often driven by revenues, this allows expenditures to be provided that will align to revenues. Administrators work to prioritize their expenditures to the budget allocation. In the event there are not enough resources for needs, from a district-wide perspective, resources can be adjusted and worked with the individual budget administrators.

## CASE STUDY: MEETING NEEDS, WANTS, AND DESIRES

Nearly every school district could have needs, wants, and desires that exceed the budget expectations. However, for the poorest of school districts, this is even more prevalent. Basic needs could not be met in a district where the tax rate was one of the highest in the state; the school district was the poorest as far as overall wealth from both a property and earned income basis. This small district had fewer than 1,500 students with a declining population. There were three elementary schools and a combined middle/high school that also housed an alternative education program.

To state that this district had unmet needs is perhaps an understatement. For example, there was paint peeling off of hallways at the middle/high school, which was four stories and had no elevator. Over 80 percent of the students qualified for free and reduced lunch.

Achievement was low, but growing. Significant measures to implement benchmark tests and improve the learning environment were in place with tutoring programs and extended core subjects. However, the performance was lower than expected.

The school district hit a year in which it experienced a significant reduction in state aid that comprised nearly 70 percent of the operating budget. There was no choice but to cut. But cut from where? The community was not vocal in providing a direction. In fact, regardless of board agenda topics, there were no members of the public present. There were no funds to broadcast the meetings.

Priorities were with academics; however, overall the administrative structure was light, with administrators carrying three and four hats relative to roles and responsibilities. Additionally, there were limited academic and extracurricular offerings to pare down. Finally, the composition of the community was residential with no business base.

There was, however, under-enrollment in the elementary buildings. A merger could probably be implemented, but what would the impact be? Would it be better to consolidate programs to improve delivery, reduce costs, and meet the needs of all students?

To even the novice, there is an assumption that reducing the number of buildings leads to reduced costs for the district. Furthermore, it would provide flexibility in instruction. Rather than three buildings that each served the same grades, one building could serve certain grades and the other serve the remaining grades to improve teacher collaboration.

- Would the consolidation of buildings be a successful way to reduce costs and save programs and staff?
- How would the community react to such a measure?
- What would the course of action look like, and how long would it take to implement?

*Chapter Four*

# Budgets as a Financial Document

One of the most complicated provisions of budgets is that they are terminology intensive. Terms like *assets*, *liabilities*, and *fund balance* are involved as critical components, and these terms have a different meaning in public sector accounting rather than private.

Bridging this gap is not only difficult but also a critical hurdle to leap over. If citizens cannot understand the fundamental components, there cannot be true active dialogue on the budget process. While certainly becoming an expert is not a requisite, a fundamental understanding of key terms and best practices can improve substantive dialogue and communication.

The approach a school district utilizes to educate the public relative to the keywords of a budget has to be gradual. For example, simply holding one session is not sufficient. A positive approach is the development of an "academy" or various intervals of educational components. If this is not feasible, other schools have utilized minor intervals of education components such as via a blog or other mechanism such as regular educational facts at meetings.

## THE STRUCTURE OF SCHOOL FINANCES

The budget of a school district should be relatively consistent in accounts and information on a year-to-year basis. In addition to an annual budget, school districts annually prepare financial statements that examine the short- and long-term finances for a district. These reports go hand in hand with the budget as prior-year performance and long-term obligations impact current and future year budgets.

In theory, there is no reason a citizen should feel daunted by the review of school financial statements. In fact, with the implementation of many required accounting standards, school district financial statements are fairly straightforward to understand. A component of each year's final financial statements is what is called a management discussion and analysis (MD&A). This document provides a summary of what has impacted a school district from year to year.

The MD&A starts with an introduction and then ordinarily reviews how the various financial statements relate to one another. Next is a presentation of summary data and analysis to explain data changes. Data are presented for the current and past fiscal year. Finally, the MD&A reviews future or current circumstances that may impact the district. For example, it may reveal important facts such as if there will be additional debt service or a new housing development that will require additional resources.

Financial performance for both past and future builds the basis for the discussion about a current-year budget. A budget is built around revenues and expenditures and a consideration of the district's fund balance that is similar to net assets in the private sector. A basic understanding of what comprises revenues and expenditures provides a good background to budget discussions.

## FUND ACCOUNTING

School districts must comply with generally accepted accounting principles, which were previously noted to differ from those in the private-sector. A core hallmark of difference is the basis of accounting. Schools operate on a modified accrual basis, which differs from the full accrual used in private-sector accounting.

The focus on modified accrual means accounting focuses on the short-term for annual financials. A component of the yearly financial reports is a reconciliation of modified accrual to full accrual; however, the daily operations focus on the modified accrual approach.

The financial statements that present the modified accrual approach provide a view of general education services. A chief characteristic of each statement is information that is presented by funds. A fund is an accounting entity created by the district for the purpose of tracking the finances of a particular group of activities. Each fund is assigned a set of assets, liabilities, and residual assets or fund balance.[1]

Every school district must have a general fund, which is where general expenditures and revenues are recorded. Additional funds are either discretionary based upon need or required by state accounting practices. Common breakouts for funds include debt service, capital projects, and an enterprise fund to record food-service revenues and expenditures.

## REVENUE CHARACTERISTICS

Revenues for a school district include those that draw from local, state, federal, and other financing sources. The composition of these revenues relative to how they create the whole revenue budget is perhaps the most important take-away. Dependent on the funding for schools, be it from a township, a state, or a combination of sources, the reliability, consistency, and ability to support the student population are critical.

In tough economic times, reliance on income and sales tax can lead to sharp decreases in these revenues, resulting from economic conditions. In better times, a reliance on a property assessment that grows with new home building and increasing home values may be advantageous to provide funding without requiring an increase in taxes. Learning your school district's composition will enable a better understanding of the revenue challenges that face the district.

Local revenues come from the direct community for which the school provides services. An example of local revenues is property tax on all properties within the boundaries of a district. Local revenues provide support that can be estimated based upon trend and other considerations such as growth in values or reduction in income if an income tax were to support the schools.

Very often districts depend on local municipalities to provide support for part or all of their programs. Regardless of whether this is the case, the link between schools and municipalities cannot be forgotten. School districts serve the municipality with a service and also provide an attraction to the community. For example, a high-performing school district with excellent facilities and numerous opportunities for students will attract families to the community.

State revenues are provided by the state in which the district exists. Often, state revenues support state initiatives such as lower class size or a minimum level of support for public education. Depending upon the state, there may be a threshold of support that is constitutionally provided. State revenues do not directly burden the community, but may draw from resources such as a sales or income tax to fund education as well as other initiatives.

Revenue from the U.S. government is called federal revenue. This revenue is provided to virtually all public school districts to support initiatives of the federal government. Examples include English as a second language and other initiatives such as professional development for staff and additional support for buildings with a higher threshold of poverty.

Federal revenues can be a small or substantial part of a budget. This is a correlation between the wealth of the district and the amount of federal revenues it receives. The correlation is as follows: the less federal money received, the wealthier the population served by the district. Commonly, the

more money received indicates a higher economically disadvantaged population served by the district, which means a higher level of federal support.

The final category that is often presented with revenues, but not considered as an annual revenue, is "other financing sources." Other financing
sources are neither revenues nor expenditures, but do impact fund balance or
net assets, which will be explained later. Other financing sources are either a
utilization of fund balance to fill a void in revenue or proceeds from a one-
time activity such as the sale of a building.

There is not an ideal composition of local, state, and federal revenues.
Perhaps from a community perspective schools that are nearly entirely locally supported can garner support as residents directly see what they pay for.
On the other hand, a reliance on state revenues rather than local may lessen
the local support monetarily for schools but also may leave the district vul-
nerable to reductions based upon state fiscal performance or other initiatives
that take political priority.

Finally, a balance may seem to be a middle of the road for revenue
composition and stability, but significant changes such as the closure of a
large employer or economic recession will still impact a district with a diver-
sified revenue source. Learning the revenue composition is nonetheless a
critical part of understanding a school district's financial picture. Community-based budgeting rests in an understanding of revenues and expenditures.
The story is very important because it relates the economics, demographics,
and other characteristics of the district.

## EXPENDITURE COMPOSITION

There is some guidance and rationale that can be provided on the classification of expenditures within a budget. Due to various state coding requirements, states often have classifications that segregate out certain costs. For
example, debt service is often segregated out from general expenditures.

Districts comply with state and federal reporting requirements for both
expenditures and revenues. What is important for the basis of community-
based budgeting is an understanding of two core components of expenditures
in each and every break out. These are functions and objects.

Functions describe the activity for which a service or material object is
acquired.[2] Functions of school districts include instruction support service,
community services, facilities, and acquisition and debt service. Each broad
function is then broken into subfunctions, which provide a classification of
activities within the function. For example, instruction is then broken into
regular education, special education, vocational education, and so on.

We have previously discussed that school districts are program-based.
The utilization of functions assists in focusing schools to track costs of pro-

gram expenditures. Functions track all associated costs with that specific activity. For example, the cost of the instructional function summarizes all costs for instruction including salary, benefits, supplies, equipment, and so on. When functional costs are compared over time, they give an indication as to what programs are costing more.

Once program costs are examined, the costs within the program are broken down into what are referred to as objects. Objects are classifications to describe the service or commodity obtained as the result of a specific expenditure.[3] Regardless of the program, the components that comprise that program or functional cost are similar. Objects not only allow a breakdown of expenditures within a program, but also provide a summary of like expenditures for a district.

For example, objects include salaries, benefits, purchased services, supplies, and equipment, to name a few. These detail the costs in each area and apply to each function. Depending upon a variety of factors, certain functions may or may not have certain objects. For example, the outsourcing of an alternative education program may lead to no associated salary and benefit cost and only a cost for the contract with the service provider.

For a district as a whole, the object costs can be summed up to provide a breakdown for the entire organization relative to the costs for individual areas such as salaries and benefits. Districts provide this information as part of the budget presentation. It is useful to examine budgets from both a functional perspective as well as an object perspective to gauge overall costs and trends in expenditures.

In an effort to provide easily understood information, the composition of expenditures may seem simple. There are many specific details within each function and breakdowns within each object that, while important, are too detailed to review within the scope of this book. States often have specific information on accounting procedures. Additionally, academic books that provide information on finance discuss expenditure breakdowns further.

## TEN MUST-KNOW TERMS

There are perhaps ten must-know terms that can be identified relative to school budgets. The understanding of these terms by the board, administration, and community as previously mentioned is critical to involving the community in the budget process. The ten terms and a basic definition are as follows[4]:

- *Assets*: What a school district owns. For example, a common asset is buildings.

- *Liabilities*: What a school district owes. For example, long-term debt service payments.
- *Fund balance*: Instead of net assets, the difference between assets and liabilities in an annual district financial report.
- *Debt service*: Payments in a current year for general long-term debt usually through bonds.
- *Reserve*: Funding set aside for an intended purpose. Most commonly seen in a budget as a "budgetary reserve."
- *Mandated expenditures*: Expenditures through laws or regulations outside of the local governing body's control to modify or adjust. An example is the requirement to comply with federal mandates for special education students.
- *Full accrual*: A basis of accounting with a "business" focus. This focus examines a full long-term perspective.
- *Modified accrual*: A basis of accounting for governments whereby revenue is recorded. This basis focuses on short-term impact.
- *Stewardship*: Spending the budget with the goal of meeting the needs and values of the community.
- *Fund*: A self-balancing set of accounts. Funds segregate governmental expenditures for transparency and ease of reporting. All school districts have at least one fund, the general fund.

## UNDERSTANDING THE FINANCIAL PLAN

Budgets are more commonly viewed to be a financial plan for a school district. The budget provides an overview of funds, accounts, and expenditure trends. While finance officials for a school district prepare a budget annually in some unified fashion, the importance of community understanding of complex financial information requires concise and understandable summaries and trends to be relayed within the final document.

When presenting a financial plan, the level of detail should be reasonable and to a level that provides information on a school's functions and a breakdown of expenditures within those functions such as salaries, benefits, supplies, and so on. (more commonly referred to as objects). This nationally accepted accounting structure provides a summary of revenues and expenditures to provide a comprehensive review of the school district's budgets.

In addition to presenting function and object information, the budget should also include information on previous years' actual expenditures, the current year's budget, and related factors relative to where the actual expenditures are compared to the budget and projections for future years. The approval of a budget for the next year is not a stand-alone process. Budget approval and direction must respond to past and future trends.

For example, passing a budget with no tax increase but not taking into account future increases for health insurance will not benefit a district long-term. Failure to address and consider significant factors and variables outside of the current year is not prudent management. Both revenues and expenditures need to be evaluated with data presented by the administration as to trends and projections.

An important consideration through the budget will be the level of routine versus non-routine expenditures. Routine expenditures include those such as salaries, benefits, utilities, and debt service. Non-routine expenditures are those that are often for one-time initiatives.

For example, an initiative of new technology is a non-routine expenditure. The expenditure is budgeted in one year and then there may be maintenance costs, but the impact to the budget is not every year. The identification of such non-routine costs paired with prudent long-term planning enables school districts to institute initiatives in various years while maintaining budget stability. The year in which the new technology is not acquired may be the year in which a new reading program is instituted.

In addition to operating funds, the budget ordinarily includes capital expenditures either as part of a pay-as-you-go function of operating expenditures or out of a separate capital budget with funds set aside for capital projects from bond funds or other sources. The amount of capital expenditures with specifics on project cost is a minimum example of information to be included relative to capital projects. Additionally, other useful information such as prioritization, life cycle analysis, and debt service should also be presented.

Of particular interest should be debt service. Contrary to common belief, debt service is actually a good indicator of a school district's ability to plan and utilize a long-term funding mechanism for immediate improvements to facilities. Too little debt service would indicate no development or facilities improvements, which may indicate that work is being put aside. Too much debt service can indicate an unnecessary burden for new facilities, which may translate into limiting resources for other categories.

The perfect balance of debt service is a level debt payment schedule with consideration for long-term needs. For example, debt is ordinarily payable over twenty to thirty years. As debt is retired, there should be a plan to take out additional debt service to meet facilities' needs. Even with a new building, after twenty years, infrastructure such as the heating, ventilation, and air conditioning unit and other systematic components will require attention. The maintenance of level debt ensures adequate resources to fund capital improvements.

There is an alternative to fund capital improvements with operating funds. While feasible and commonly referenced as a pay-as-you-go financing plan, this method provides annual operating expenditures earmarked and identified for improvements. Unfortunately, in light of increasing mandates, rising costs, and declining revenues at various intervals, pay-as-you-go funding is often susceptible to be reduced and adversely impacts infrastructure.

In other words, expenditures within a budget that are not necessary are often reduced to meet more pressing needs. A common argument is: Can't a major project wait until next year? You can probably even finish this scenario, as in the next year, it becomes pushed to the next year and then is never addressed until a critical point in which it is not feasible for further reduction. In a pay-as-you-go funding mechanism, the budgetary impact is significant in the final year in which the project is at a point that it has to be addressed.

## CASE STUDY: SIMPLIFYING THE COMPLEX

One of the most challenging tasks associated with budget preparation is the dissemination of information in a clear and concise manner. From time to time, I have heard my colleagues mention that one number or one visual explains the budget completely.

While a single number such as a deficit may make a point relative to the situation, there must be an explanation of certain trends and impacts. For example, it could be asked, what is driving the deficit? Additionally, there needs to be context. In light of the terms defined earlier in this chapter, they lend to the overall financial condition.

Proactive clarification and information can work at times to dispel myths relative to a situation. For example, providing fund balance information can improve the understanding of the overall financial situation and explain long-term impacts of its utilization.

- Select a term from the ten outlined. Focus on the one you feel is most important. Hard to decide? Select two or three of the terms that are most important and contemplate why you believe they are such.
- Are there any missing terms that you have heard your local school board discuss?

## NOTES

1. Mead, Dean Michael. *What You Should Know about Your School District's Finances.* Norwalk, CT: Governmental Accounting Standards Board, 2000. 25.
2. Allison, Gregory, Honegger, Steven D., Johnson, Frank, and Hoffman, Lee. *Financial Accounting for Local and State School Systems: 2009 Edition.* Washington, DC: National Center for Educational Statistics, Institute of Education Sciences, U.S. Department of Education, 2009. 113.
3. Allison, Gregory, Honegger, Steven D., Johnson, Frank, and Hoffman, Lee. *Financial Accounting for Local and State School Systems: 2009 Edition.* Washington, DC: National

Center for Educational Statistics, Institute of Education Sciences, U.S. Department of Education, 2009. 125.

4.  Mead, Dean Michael. *What You Should Know about Your School District's Finances.* Norwalk, CT: Governmental Accounting Standards Board, 2000. 5–10.

# Chapter Five

# Budgets as an Operational Document

A district's budget provides information on programs such as expenditures for regular versus special education, athletic and extracurricular costs, and debt service and contracted service costs. Additionally, best practices recommend including detail on enrollment, demographics, and test scores. The inclusion of this information provides an overview of the performance results associated with the fiscal plan in prior and current years.

The impact of state mandates is ordinarily outlined in a budget document. Mandates are not fully funded from other levels of government. Addressing this in a budget notates the impact from a fiscal standpoint as well as the way in which the district is meeting those mandates.

For example, the school district may note that its mandates are from certain requirements for special education. Additionally, there may be a portion of funding for said mandates, but more often than not, there is a lack of funding. The school district ordinarily will discuss the impact of mandates and the associated expenditures relative to providing an appropriate program.

From an operational perspective, there is a presentation of trends, benchmarks, and other unique items in the district's operating structure. For example, personnel costs may be misaligned with other districts due to a direct hire of all staff on an in-house rather than contracting out basis. Moreover, there may be purchases driven by program needs for technology that no matter the economics need to be purchase to improve achievement and/or to provide relief from purchasing traditional textbooks.

## ORGANIZATIONAL STRUCTURE

The structure of an organization is the direct link between the school district and individual departments or buildings. Budgets must take into consideration these components to demonstrate stewardship and responsibility. School district operating structures vary. With budgets being driven at least in part by input from sites and departments, they are then combined at a broader level to demonstrate a cohesive and organized plan.

A budget will show the organizational structure and information on staffing. A best practice is to include information on previous staffing levels and to denote significant variables and discrepancies that will change in the upcoming budget.

Based upon local impact, information on retirements, trends in hiring, and experience of teachers may also be provided. The goal with discussing the organizational structure is not only to paint a picture of the school, but to provide substantive yet clear information on the budget and how staffing is impacted.

## BUDGETS IN DAY-TO-DAY ADMINISTRATION OF EDUCATION

A side that is not often seen publicly, but which is the case in every school that operates under a budget, is the impact on day-to-day operations. Decisions such as adding a teacher to reduce class size, what to do about overcrowding on a school bus, and how to accommodate the needs of new students all rest in an ultimate decision that can be positive, negative, or neutral in impact to the budget.

A budget is ordinarily approved once a year, but the education of students is a fluid process. Students, once enrolled, may separate due to movement factors such as family migrations or new housing developments within the district. Additionally, there may be an ability to reduce staff based on lower enrollments, but then enrollments spike. Adjustments are inevitable and can be made through a balance of needs versus wants.

Additionally, there is a reporting mechanism whereby in most schools, monthly if not quarterly financial reports are presented and the administration discusses or notes variances or obstacles. In a quest to make budgets more understandable, many school districts are migrating to a point where they are implementing data dashboards and other information that is easily interpreted on financial positions.

Furthermore, the daily impact of the budget on programs challenges the administrative team to seek ways to reduce costs even beyond the budget cycle. For example, the purchase of supplies at less than anticipated funds may allow a previously denied request for technology to be approved. Additionally, an unanticipated price increase may prove to be an opportunity for the business official to research costs and solicit quotations or bids to maintain a competitive pricing structure.

Finally, the advent of meeting needs requires a constant search for additional revenues beyond local, state, and federal funds. More recently, school districts have looked to their community to provide ideas for alternative revenue generation, be it through user fees, donations, grants, or tax credits. Alternative funds can vary from year to year but can provide a source of income otherwise unavailable.

## BUDGETS AS PRIORITY-SETTING MODELS

Both in the development and implementation of the budget, a school district has the ability to establish priorities. Priorities are set through a formal priority setting process that includes the following steps:

- Step 1: Identify issues
- Step 2: Identify goals to address issues
- Step 3: Establish objectives for goals
- Step 4: Evaluate programs and projects
- Step 5: Develop budget work plans

In the first step, issues are prioritized based on the school district's process to identify areas of concern. Issues can be identified from a variety of means such as hearings, focus groups, surveys, and meetings. Following the identification process, a prioritization is made. Often, priorities are set based on values, plans, policies, and programs or projects that have been evaluated from a quantitative or qualitative perspective.

In step two, goals are established to determine what a project or program will achieve. For example, a goal may be to eliminate the achievement gap. The third step builds on the goal and determines how the goal will be accomplished by establishing an objective. For example, an objective to bridge the achievement gap is to hire a consultant to prepare a recommendation report. Objectives must be concrete deliverables that provide a foundation to achieve the goal.

The fourth step is where the budget factors in significantly. Within this second to last step, options must be chosen. Which plans to pursue to accomplish the objectives should be identified. There may be multiple ways to achieve goals and various means relative to costs. For example, the ability to hire a consultant may be one way to achieve the goal, but perhaps building capacity through a train-the-trainer model is a better route that over the long-term may reduce residual costs.

Often, options are evaluated for cost both for the current year as well as future years. A best cost/benefit ratio is often utilized to determine the balance between achieving results and judiciously spending funds. The cost/

benefit ratio takes into account the cost for an initiative compared to the benefit. To a point funds can improve the outcome or benefit, but there is a leveling off where additional expenditures do not necessarily increase the benefits.

The goal of the budget is to meet objectives while working within budget restrictions. The next step is a budget work plan. The budget work plan is the alignment of financial factors to the priorities. Often, the work plan may change based upon delivery variables. Additionally, the work plan may span multiple years, which is often a way to address a pressing need with limited financial resources. Multi-year planning is a perfect demonstration of recognizing needs and preparing action steps via objectives.

## COMMUNITY INVOLVEMENT IN THE OPERATIONAL COMPONENT

The argument can be made that the operational component of a budget is predominantly an administrative function. This process of identifying goals and assigning objectives is based on feedback and data received on a daily basis from community interactions. Often unperceived in this manner, routine feedback from assessments and community input via parent and community groups all become factors for consideration in developing goals and generating options for objectives.

Additionally, the strategic planning process that is performed by most districts is a process that involves participation from stakeholders. The involvement of stakeholders that includes administration, faculty, students, parents, businesses, and community members is a valuable component to defining short- and long-term goals.

Outside of the strategic planning process, community involvement in the operational and priority-setting components of a budget process must be integrated with ongoing district means for decision-making and community relations. For example, utilizing parent teacher organization meetings to provide information and receive feedback are more valuable than scheduling a standalone meeting on the same topic.

Additionally, committee structures and other components are areas in which input is often received on various initiatives. Again, incorporating citizen feedback and citizens taking an active role in ongoing operational needs is what propels the organization forward without being bogged down in standalone components.

Finally, citizens must realize that involvement entails more than simply coming out strong on standalone issues or even only as a budget is moved into a final stage. Involvement must be ongoing in part to understand the culture and important factors for consideration in the decision-making process. Decisions are not made upon financials alone. There is always a backbone to decisions that is contained in the organization's goals and objectives

## CASE STUDY: ADMINISTRATORS WORKING WITHIN BUDGET CONSTRAINTS

As previously discussed, budgets are passed and then the administration moves into an implementation phase relative to the budget. In this case, budget projections and the identification of needs are aligned to a reality. Very often, the projections are on target with the actual situation at hand. At certain times, however, there are unintended consequences.

With the economic downturn, school district budgets have no doubt become tighter and tighter. Budgets are based on assumptions for both revenues and expenditures, but required mandates and variables contribute uncertainty to the exactness of making expenditures balance with revenue streams.

For one school district, the budget was passed. There were appropriate provisions for a projected increase in enrollment. Enrollment increased as projected, but then the fact that a new building opened meant that the registrations surpassed budgetary plans. Additionally, utilities from a market perspective were exceeding projections as well. Finally, mandated costs for special education were increasing merely through identification and needs to provide appropriate programs for all students. In the simplest sense, the rising expenditures were unable to be controlled without eliminating the category.

The challenge to meet needs despite limited resources was significant. More challenging than many other types of governmental budgets, there are of course labor contracts and other contracted services such as alternative placements and facility maintenance agreements. Additionally, modifications have an immediate impact to the process. For example, combining transportation routes not only impacts students, but impacts parents and their schedules.

The administration met to review the situation and evaluate options. It was determined that there were three options that could be taken. The first option was to increase class size by one student to alleviate the need to add an additional professional staff member. Additionally, operating expenditures would be reviewed and a reduction would be made on any spending that was not categorized as necessary in light of the circumstances at this point in time.

The second option was to utilize the fund balance: the district had a below average amount saved. However, in light of the fact that the cost for an additional teacher including benefits and the other expenditures was

$175,000 on a $125,000,0000 budget, this was a path that could accommodate needs without any budgetary impact.

A third option was to examine support staff positions and reduce where possible. Reducing positions that were classified as full time with benefits to part time was an option. Reducing them to a status where the positions would not qualify for benefit was a secondary option. Each position for which this was accomplished for would save $14,500. The administration believed there could be five positions for which this may be feasible, achieving savings of $72,500.

To accommodate the additional expenditures, the school district would look to reduce its activity buses one day each week (probably Monday as it was a lightly used day). This option would save thirty-three thousand dollars over the course of a year. Other reductions in the same manner as discussed in scenario one with reducing operating expenditures in light of the aforementioned circumstances are no longer a priority for the district.

- While none of the options are desirable, which ones would you select?
- What would be the basis for your decision?
- How would you justify your answer in consideration of the need to balance meeting student needs with finite resources?

*Chapter Six*

# Budgets as a Policy Document

One of the primary roles and purposes of most school boards is to establish policy. Policies provide a framework for the administration. Policy is developed to provide goals and objectives as well as parameters for operating to administer the educational program. Budgets serve as a fundamental way of implementing policy and providing information on policies and procedures that impact the budget.

The majority of policy decisions involve fiscal implications to one or more areas of the educational organization. For example, a decision to implement full-day preschool or kindergarten impacts fiscal costs for staffing, transportation, and building operations.

Therefore, policy cannot be developed without an analysis of the fiscal implications. Additionally, as a governing board, policy decisions cannot be implemented through the budget without being vetted through the board and public review process.

## SCHOOL POLICIES

School district policies are ordinarily developed and approved by the board after several periods of review and public comment. School policies provide supporting information to cover federal and state laws and codes to provide a framework for school operations. Based upon the policy, the school district then develops administrative regulations to guide implementation.

School policies reflect ideologies of the board and community through the feedback process. While the budget has fiscal implications from policies, there also should be policies to govern budget development. Examples of policies to govern budget development include the following:

- Fiscal objectives
- Fund balance
- Budgetary reserve
- Budget planning, preparation, and adoption
- Other polies that broadly govern budget development and implementation

Through the development of policies, the school district is able to establish various parameters and direction for the budget process. It is quite possible these could include community involvement. More often depending upon annual circumstances, community involvement is probably best outlined in the annual budget calendar and as an overall organizational component in annual processes and events.

## BUDGETS AS A PLAN AND ROADMAP

A school district's budget is a plan for how resources will be allocated. Based on various needs, wants, and desires, the budget represents the plan to meet various goals and objectives. The budget is a policy document of the priorities and intentions of upcoming and prior fiscal years.

Ordinarily, the board approves a school district's budget. In the course of developing the budget, the administration, board, and community develop how to meet needs and address wants and desires. The budget is less about the numbers as a story and more about the records of information.

The budget serves at functions[1] including:

- A record of the past: It reflects decisions and actions taken in previous budgets to narrate the impact. For example, history in the budget will reveal decisions to augment or reduce programs and the associated expenditures.
- A statement of the future: It relays information on the future outlook both for the district economically and programmatically based on the decisions that are made. The budget is a catalyst for critical decisions. For example, the inclusion of debt service speaks to the desire to improve existing facilities.
- Predictions of future actions: The budget provides information on what direction the district will pursue in the future. For example, noting that taxes are among the highest in a state may indicate a desire to maintain current tax rates to provide relief from a perceived burden or a justification of what the local taxes support.
- A mechanism for allocating resources: Funds are allocated based on needs, wants, and desires. The budget reflects that in light of the limited nature of funding, the school district is striving to allocate based on an

identification of priorities. The increased costs as a result of mandated expenditures speak to the need to address federal mandates over which the district has no control.

## BUDGETS AS A COMMUNICATION DOCUMENT

School budgets are often known to communicate priorities, but they also serve as a communication vehicle for the district as a whole. The budget is an opportunity to discuss progress with the strategic plan and educational and operational objectives and accomplishments.

Due to the fact that budgets draw the public's attention, it is an excellent communication venue to frame the financials of the district. In fact, it can become a blueprint to the community relative to charting the course not only for the next year, but reviewing prior year accomplishments and future objectives.

The budget can be a tool to provide strategic information to the community. As the budget is part of an annual approval and vetting process, it is a way for a district to highlight achievements and accomplishments. School budgets reflect the community and their values. The budget can also showcase opportunities for students and the involvement of parents and stakeholders in the community. The production of various components of a larger budget document not only provides information on the impact of policies for the district, it also informs and provides the link between stewardship and student achievement.

## BUDGET REQUESTS REFLECT POLICY GUIDELINES

Drawing from the role that policies guide budget development, there are impacts on budgeting from policies. Even the simplest policy that mandates volunteer background checks at the expense of the board of education could impact budget expenditures. Most policies positively or negatively impact revenues or expenditures. Policies therefore directly impact the budget and set the parameters for future revenue and expenditure increases or decreases.

More commonly, policies on class size, transportation, debt management, and other larger-scale areas are those that have substantial budget impact. Adding to board policy, contracts entered by the board impact budget. Drawing from the fact that for most districts personnel and benefits are the most costly resources, negotiations become crucial. Contracted agreements between the board of directors and staff are formal statements. These agreements reflect the board's philosophy and how areas such as class size, number of work days, and length of work year translate to fiscal implications.

In recent economic times, labor negotiations are where districts may be able to make inroads, explain economics, benchmark data, and settle contractual expenditure trends. Consideration of these points can make a significant impact to a district's long-term fiscal stability. Aside from economic givebacks, school districts work to improve operational efficiency in policy modifications.

We often think of how contract negotiations drive expenditures, but with assessments to employees for benefits, there is the opportunity to receive revenue from employees for their healthcare. In light of rising healthcare costs often trending in double digits, districts have easily surpassed seven figures in contributions to offset core health plans.

## BUDGET ALIGNS LEGISLATIVE ACTIONS TO FISCAL REALITY

Boards of education are charged with implementing not only fiscal policies, but polices that support programs, pupils, employees, finances property, operations, and the community. Policies that support worthwhile initiatives such as volunteers and payment to a local library are well intended; however, there are undoubtedly fiscal implications. Legislative prioritization of top policies guide budget development and translate into fiscal allocations.

Very often in response to fiscal crises, policies are changed. For example, class size is increased, walking distances to bus stops are increased, or other measures to increase revenues are put into place, such as developing prices for naming rights or implementing pay to play. The modification of policies can positively impact the fiscal reality and can preserve draconian cuts such as sports or extracurricular activities.

A forward-thinking board will seek to modify policies prior to the need to respond to fiscal issues. Additionally, policies relative to fund balance and reserves as already discussed are critical parameters for the development of the budget.

Additionally, all legislative actions, be they hiring staff, retirements, costs for capital projects, or awards of bid, all come together in the budget. There is the current impact and the projected impact. For example, a trend to hire staff regardless of experience level will impact projections for budget. A commitment to hire staff at an initial cap will drive projections in a different way.

In addition to staffing levels, budgets discuss short-term initiatives and long-term goals that will impact fiscal or organizational operation. The impact of legislation from both state and federal mandates are policy decisions that while out of control of the local governing body can be reviewed.

# CASE STUDY: POLICY LINKS TO BUDGET PRIORITIES

The link between policy and budget is perhaps one of the best representations that the budget is not a standalone once-a-year event. Policies that are vetted for community input become a basis for budget development. Policies are often confused with procedures. Policies set broad-based authority and positions from which the superintendent can promulgate guidelines and the administration can implement.

With the onset of support for charter schools, many districts have developed their own charter schools be they cyber or brick and mortar. The view is often that if the public wants such an option, the district should cater and provide appropriately. The reaction in this manner is that often when students leave an educational system, the system's funding is lost. Schools are unable to reduce costs until the loss of students is at a certain level where staff, buses, and other costs can be reduced.

Many districts have developed policies to permit these alternative programs. While the decision to offer may seem simple, there are startup costs that take money away from other programs. Additionally, there is an award of a diploma for those who complete the program that may be viewed to be equal to these students who successfully complete a traditional educational experience. This is not always the case.

A district was in a decision-making process weighing the pros and cons of instituting a cyber school. Establishment of a cyber school would mean that the district would attract those students who sought this learning experience and would keep local funds local so that the district would not lose funds to another entity. It was proposed that students would earn a local diploma, yet it would note that is was from the district's cyber academy.

A counter argument to implementing a cyber charter was the fact that to some, it seemed that the district would compromise the educational reputation it held at a national level through the implementation of a cyber charter. Arguments were presented that implementing a cyber program would not prepare students and the presentation of a diploma would be perceived to be equivalent to that from a brick and mortar school, which would be misleading.

Despite the various arguments, there was a need for cost savings and maintenance of revenue locally. This was a viable, accepted option to the greater community. In light of the philosophical arguments against the program, the fact that the program needed to be instituted was almost a natural endpoint.

In consideration of the options, a decision was made to not proceed with the program. For the administration, this was a decision that impacted budget, but the board had made up their minds on the matter. There was no way to change.

As a result, the school district had increased the net cost of charter students by 30 percent in the future year. As a result, there had to be reductions in expenditures elsewhere to balance the budget.

- Would you support the decision in this manner?
- What could have been an alternative decision?
- What impacts would this have on the district?

## NOTE

1. Wood, R. Craig. *School District Budgeting. Principles of School Business Management.* Reston, VA: Association of School Business Officials International, 1986. 12-2–12-7. Print.

*Chapter Seven*

# Public Perception and Expectations

There is often a skewed public perception relative to school budgets. A few common misconceptions include the following: school budgets are wasteful, full of overpaid administrators, not forward thinking, and have too much fat to be reduced. Regardless of addressing these concerns from an offensive and defensive condition, without true involvement of the community and an educational component, the perceptions will not change.

In most districts, eliminating the entire administrative team including building-based staff would reduce roughly a miniscule percentage of a budget, usually close to a percent or two. Some examples of public perceptions relative to anti-administrators are easily found in numerous news releases, which neglect the critical role of a viable forward-thinking administrative team.

Despite the perception of the public, the expectations of constituents runs a wide spectrum from high-quality programs utilizing scarce sources of funding to essential programs with a variety of funding sources. There are more adverse perceptions of school budgets than positive. Very often, the sentiment is only relayed about a budget process in difficult economic situations. Be it a tax increase, program cuts, or other additional measures that are contrary to the normal ebb and flow of program operations, the community will rally.

The rally is usually a reaction to a situation for which the "train has already left the station" or a prophecy of sorts has already come to fruition. Community involvement in the budget process is a component that can maintain awareness in both good and bad times. Additionally, to those who are not directly vested in schools, this process can maintain recognition of an effective administration to reduce costs and direct resources to programs.

## TAXES: WHAT ARE YOU GETTING?

School districts provide a service: education. Similar to having a contractor build a home, there is an associated cost with the desired program or size of the house which is built. The parallels to household expenditures cease at this point. Schools are required to educate children based on revenue from a wide reach of the community or state. There is not a tangible concept that paying out a certain amount of money means something is received in return.

Community welfare, well-being, and good are components whereby education is perceived similarly to developing great highways to benefit even those not directly utilizing the school system at that point in time. However, highways are visible, even parks are visible. All too often schools are not visible except to those currently utilizing the service.

Moreover, there is not a direct correlation relative to what may be able to be seen in schools that may include strong academic achievement and varied opportunities to serve all students and the tax impact to the individual. It is an impossible task to correlate taxes to what each member of a community receives. A better correlation is the stewardship component, which means that funds are allocated based on a priority rather than a scattered manner.

## USING THE PRESS

Very often, the press, including blogs, websites, newspapers, television, and radio, is negative towards public education. With the advent of technology, utilizing the media to benefit the school district is easier than ever. Information on the district's website and other additional stories relative to highlights can boost a district's reputation as well as serves to inform the entire community about the successes.

While this seems common sense, from a perspective of budget, districts are often more concerned with the process rather than the press. It falls to reporter inquiries often tipped off by citizens for information to be reported to the public outside of meetings and the district's website. Forward-thinking release of information in small doses is a viable strategy to inform and address issues that may surface.

Pushing out information both before, during, and after budget approval is a favorable strategy. Not only does it maintain awareness about the process, but it also shows the multiple facets of budgeting and impact. For example, information on budget reductions outside of the budget cycle can demonstrate to the community dedication to efficiencies.

Additionally, outside of the written word, visibility and rapport with constituents is critical to information sharing. To the extent possible, meeting parents, community groups, and those who are proposing ideas in public meetings can only serve to benefit the district and the board and administration's successful management of programmatic needs and budgetary requirements.

## STAKEHOLDERS

The budget process has many stakeholders and they fall into the following groups: community, school board, administrators, other school staff, and students. The following chart shows how these groups fit into the various stages of the budget process.

This process is one in which community involvement at various intervals is critical, yet it has to be from informed citizens who maintain a reasonable level of involvement and awareness of the issues facing education. The com-

**Table 7.1.**

|  | Community | School Board | Administrators | Other School Staff | Students |
|---|---|---|---|---|---|
| Needs assessment | X | X | X | X | X |
| Review policy and procedures |  | X |  |  |  |
| Establish educational goals |  | X | X |  |  |
| Establish program objectives |  |  | X | X |  |
| Establish support services goals |  |  | X | X |  |
| Establish support services objectives |  |  | X | X |  |
| Identify constraints for program and support services |  |  | X | X |  |
| Develop alternatives | X | X | X | X | X |
| Decide on recommendations |  | X | X |  |  |
| Confirm resource availability |  |  | X | X |  |
| Monitor programs | X | X | X | X | X |
| Evaluate programs |  |  | X | X |  |
| Future planning | X | X | X | X | X |

munity should therefore be involved at the onset and other critical milestones during the process as well as in monitoring and future planning.

There is a delicate balance between the community, board, and administration. The community provides ongoing input and feedback into the budget process. This feedback is essential in the development of a budget that meets the needs and represents the values of the community.

The school board establishes policies and goals in concert with the administration. The board works on these policies on an ongoing basis that includes reviewing old policies and establishing new policies for the administration to work within.

The administration works with the board, community, staff, and students to ensure the most appropriate allocation of resources. The administration is charged with developing cost reduction ideas and program oversight to maximize student achievement.

Other school staff are both involved and yet often disconnected from the budget process. For example, staff may submit specific budget requests to an administrator, but may not be ordinarily involved in the budget process. A critical component of the budget cycle is for staff to submit requests that will meet the program goals and objectives.

Reductions just to meet a target will impact programs more adversely than those reductions that will still enable goal accomplishments. Additionally, there is the need for school-based staff to develop alternatives to how programs can be delivered.

Student voice is an often forgotten perspective. Students can provide substantial feedback and evaluation of the budget process and impact. Understanding the reality that faces education is also important for instituting the need for involvement not only by the students but their parents who can subsequently be drawn in as advocates in the process.

## COMMUNITY EXPECTATIONS

A district that borders a large urban school district faced some critical decisions. The school had over 80 percent of its students from an economically disadvantaged black population. Furthermore, the district had a fledgling white population that was holding on to years gone by. There was clearly a shift in demographics and expectations.

The school had one of the highest tax rates in the state and concurrently one of the lowest reliance on local revenues of any district in the state. There was a clear struggle to balance aging infrastructure with necessary instructional programs and ongoing interventions to improve academic performance.

While there was an elected school board, there was little public involvement in the direction of the schools. Furthermore, due to the economic environment, decisions were made based on a pure fiscal basis and not necessarily a program reality. For example, while there was an intent to provide opportunities to meet the needs of all students, from time to time, there was the need to reduce costs to balance the budget.

In a community such as this, what is the community's expectations? Often, desired outcomes grow from community members looking for results fueled by perception or from their desire to justify taxation. Community expectations must be met to perpetuate a cycle of support and move the school district forward.

Meeting expectations, however, does not equate to responding to individual community member demands. Meeting expectations involves listening to all feedback and then appropriately moving forward on that which is best for students and responds to the community as a whole in their expectations.

## TAXATION AND EXPECTATIONS

Community expectations are often fueled by the tax burden paid or going to be paid. Very often, budgetary decisions are made in light of the impact to the community via some form of taxation, be it at a state or local level. Additionally, for those with individuals in a school system, they want to maximize the opportunities their children will receive for the taxes paid. For those with no specific interest in the school system, there is a desire to minimize burden for a service they do not use.

Even middle of the road or lower tax–rated communities become aware of the impact and desire to maintain status quo. There is no indifference to taxation purely from the fact that a community has a lower tax burden. An increase is an increase, and it plays out within the budget with program elimination or modification at mercy.

Community-based budgeting is even more important in light of taxation. Decisions made cannot be purely monetary and cannot be purely programmatic. There has to be not only a balance, but also a plan to meet ongoing needs. Long-term planning is one of the most important aspects of budgeting, and a long-term plan can only be developed with opportunities for input from the community at large regardless of involvement levels with the school district specifically.

## CASE STUDY: OUTSOURCING TO REDUCE BUDGET IMPACT

In tough economic times, one of the most significant areas a school district can look to reduce costs is in the area of salaries and benefits. A school district examined this area relative to the outsourcing of support staff, which included research on what areas would be most advantageous.

The district looked at the implications of all areas of support staff including cafeteria, transportation, custodial, academic, and clerical staff. The immediate conclusion was the most significant savings could be achieved through the outsourcing of transportation operations. The district began the negotiations process and bargained while also seeking proposals to provide transportation services.

During the course of the process, an up swell of community unrest came to the forefront. Concerns were raised relative to the current quality of service provided and the ability of an outside party to deliver the same level of service. Additionally, the bonds between students and parents and the bus drivers brought an immediate defense of current wage structure and benefits.

Despite the best efforts to reduce costs and to pursue the process in fairness and merely as a response to economic constraints and not dissatisfaction in service, there seemed to be an inability to win from any direction. The possible paths seemed to include the following:

- Continue with the bid for service, upsetting the community while providing fiscal prudence and budget relief.
- Halt the process and give up the budgetary relief, which was so needed in limiting increases on property taxes.

- Considering this information and the situation, what solutions to the issue could be reached?
- What obstacles exist to a resolution that appeals to all parties?

*Chapter Eight*

# Identify Your Community

The purpose of this book is to provide a universal platform and generalized ideas for community involvement; there is not necessarily a one-size-fits-all solution. Communities vary in economic, social, and demographic components. These three factors significantly drive the design, composition, and programs of the representative school district.

Economic factors are what most school districts are commonly defined by, which are often wealthy, economically disadvantaged, or somewhere in between. These characteristics are often unchangeable over a short or long time period. Therefore, they provide an essential lens through which to examine the community's needs, wants, and desires.

Economic factors are personal income as well as market value, which equates to property values. From these two broad indicators are many subindicators such as employment and relationship of residential to commercial properties. These indicators can be compared to regional, state, and national factors to gauge where a community ranks.

Determining what economic situation a school community is impacted by can be gleaned from the rising or declining incomes or market values. For example, those communities on the lower economic spectrum may be more or less impacted as a result of economic unrest or progress.

Social refers to the composition of the community. Ethnicity, age, and other characteristics determine the programs that a school may need to deliver. Education as a program cannot be delivered as a one-size-fits-all solution. Programs must reflect the social needs of the students and communities served.

While schools ordinarily provide core programs for children in grades kindergarten through senior high, they can provide supplemental programs for both revenue and community relations purposes to various needs in the population. For example, in a district that has a growing retiree population, there may be opportunities to have utilization of the district's library media centers or even form an adult school that will provide not only opportunities but serve to continue to engage the community.

Demographic refers to the characteristics of the community. What is the average age, household composition, or profession? Is this a community of professionals who seek to provide world class opportunities or a program that provides core programs rather than more diverse offerings?

Throughout the United States, there are numerous schools whose communities take pride in the variety and number of programs offered. On the opposite end of the spectrum, there are those schools that provide core functions and supplemental opportunities through outside means.

Minding the demographic and social needs assists in the prioritization previously discussed in the book. Prioritization frequently relates back to the social, economic, and demographic characteristics. These characteristics are also why benchmark comparisons, while valuable, are not always data that represents a school's specific composition. Therefore, this appearance may not provide solid comparisons on costs and revenues.

An emphasis for members of the public as part of community-based budgeting is to be mindful of the characteristics that define the school district and represent all students. Communities are composed of neighborhoods that have their own various populations and demographics which make up the district as a whole. The district must strive to meet the needs of all students with limited economic means.

## IDENTIFY WITH THOSE OUTSIDE THE SCHOOL

Of course, economic, social, and demographic characteristics do not only represent those who the schools directly serve, but also those devoid of any involvement in the schools. For example, retirees or a younger population significantly impact and subsequently should drive the considerations in community-based budgeting.

Often, these "disconnected" constituents can be reached outside of the normal school functions through community or political groups. Additionally, these can be supporters of various standalone components of a school district. For example, an organization may be the Rotary or another social service organization in your vicinity.

In addition to serving as an advocate, the constant support of outside organizations is critical to not only ensure success and reach out to all constituents with a vested interest in the school, but to build support. For example, small bits and pieces of information that are provided to outsiders at regular intervals will only serve to continue to lend credibility and support to the school district in more trying times.

## WORKING TOGETHER FOR STUDENT SUCCESS

Administrators, school board members, and the community want the school district to succeed, but also want individual student success for each and every student serviced. Working together on fiscal, operational, and educational issues is a critical step in the process. Similar to the success in other fields, working together becomes a critical component. Pitting parents against a school board only stalls progress. While disagreement and various thoughts are encouraged, there should be a desire to come together, once various points have been debated, on a plan that incorporates the best course of action from all input received.

Perhaps a striking example that has stood out in the minds of those in the business world is the fall of the steel industry. It is perhaps a "modern" example of how despite any record of success, when two sides (union and management) cannot come together, success cannot continue. Additionally, a failure to consider the bigger picture can be problematic. Not incorporating how decisions fit into goals and objectives can lead to failure. For example, union wages and a failure to adapt to changes in steel were contributing factors in the demise of the industry.

The demise of the steel industry has many parallels to how school districts cannot work without their community in propelling student achievement to higher levels such as those in certain areas in other countries. Communities and school districts must work together to ensure continued and improved success of all students.

Working together begins with trust. A foremost characteristic, trust is not considered in light of ongoing calls for transparency and various other political party agendas. Education is a people business. Students are served, staff employed, and communities (made of people) are to be engaged. Trust is critical as an ongoing need to ensure continued success in good times and to collaborate in bad times.

Not only the district's administrators and board, but all staff must connect with the community and champion the school district. Beyond the district, businesses and other community organizations must be engaged and trust in what steps the district is taking while providing feedback and support. Very often, the trust is built gradually and built upon regular updates and information sharing. In an informal setting such as meeting with community groups or sharing district highlights, trust can be better developed.

# CASE STUDY: IDENTIFY WITH THOSE INSIDE AND OUTSIDE YOUR SCHOOLS

A school district that bordered a large urban center was in a significant change of population. Once a traditionally upper middle class population, the school district was now receiving an increase in its economically disadvantaged population due to a flee from poorly performing schools in the city and a desire by parents of economically disadvantaged students to move out of the city to a school district that provided significantly improved educational opportunities such as art, music, and drama.

The school district population was unprepared for the transition. While the administration knew the measures that needed to be taken, certain factions of the board and a vocal portion of the population wanted to hold on to what the school district had been. There was a constant struggle between meeting the needs of all students the district served. The vocal parents created a community where each and every decision was the result of emotional toil to maintain status quo.

The district superintendent began a series of community conversations. These conversations revolved around a series of incidents at the high school. There was a lower than previously experienced caliber of students attending and graduating from the high school. Internally, discussions were held with faculty and staff to review concerns. Additionally, there was outreach to various civic and religious organizations to relay the good work the school district had been trying to accomplish.

Committees were formed for everything from the achievement gap to female violence to mentoring. The approach was highly reactive and sought to address the vocal minority and those involved with the schools while ignoring any proactive measures. The unspoken goal of each committee was to review the topic and provide venue for discussion to deter anyone feeling as if they were not heard.

- Was this measure successful in drawing together the community?
- In light of the need for the budget to reflect the community, would the measures described here be enough to maintain focused and succinct spending to meet the needs of all students?

## Chapter Nine

# Various Forms of Community-based Budgeting

Community-based budgeting, like many other processes, can take on many forms. The root of working with a community to meet their goals is to understand not only the demographics of the community as far as expectations, needs, wants, and desires, but also what community members (as far as a representation of all interests) should be drawn into the budget process.

Before we can begin to discuss the process of drawing members in, the first step is to discuss models of members and their various involvement degrees. A grid can provide us with information relative to the various stages of involvement. Review this grid from the bottom to the top to have insight into the stages a citizen's involvement can take.

The categories in Table 9.1 imply that synergistic is the top involvement level for community members. There are those community members, however, who not only over-involve themselves and ultimately their coalitions, but will work against the administration to achieve their personal objectives. Over-involvement can also intimidate those who may desire to become more involved.

Unlike a disgruntled or irrational resident who begins in opposition to the process, synergistic individuals begin in support of their school district. They champion education. However, once the tide turns and political or policy decisions have followed an engagement process, these groups may utilize their level of involvement to oppose the process.

Irrational community members are often the most destructive type of community member. In this category, residents are educated to a point, but often egos or ulterior motives, such as preserving a change in the community, feed into their position.

**Table 9.1.   Levels of Involvement**

| | |
|---|---|
| **Synergistic** | Involvement and interest in collaboratively working with those who are in policy and administrative roles |
| **Active** | Citizen who recognizes the need to exercise his or her role in shaping the direction of a school district |
| **Passive-Active** | Constituent who is aware of issues and engages in the political or citizen-driven processes |
| **Passive** | Resident neither interested in happenings nor concerned about the school system or local legislative process |
| **Disgruntled** | Taxpayer who is dissatisfied with the services of the school |
| **Irrational** | Member of the community who misrepresents understanding of global events, statistics, and policy decisions to prove an unfounded point |

Within all of these personas, how do you find your place in the community? For example, many of us will not place ourselves permanently into one category. We may waft from being disgruntled at times that there is a tax increase to being synergistic with tough budget decisions.

The point is not necessarily where you fit, but rather an awareness of where you stand and where you tend to go. Often knowing where you will land heightens your confidence to consider or ponder key issues before tackling the issues.

## FROM THE SCHOOL PERSPECTIVE

There are many legal requirements school districts must follow. As a general rule, many school systems require a public advertising and inspection period. This enables proper review of budget and fiscal documents. But complying with such requirements is merely an attempt of the district to meet the mandates. Much more can be done for community input and feedback, and to improve understanding of the process.

There are many school districts across the nation that exceed requirements relative to community feedback and input into the budget process. For example, community forums are just one venue in which school districts exceed mandated requirements. Other outreach efforts can include discussions with parent organizations, teachers, and community leaders.

School districts that truly look for community-driven input and assumptions are dynamic in not only how they operate, but also how they meet the needs of their community. Input, feedback, and involvement are not only critical to the cyclical process.

## FROM A PUBLIC PERSPECTIVE

It may seem as no surprise that the public desires to have an abundance of top-notch programs at the lowest cost to the individual who has to pay whatever taxing mechanism may be in place. Interestingly, however, there are communities where the value in programs equates to the attractiveness for families to the school system.

Perhaps the most difficult perspective comes from those who are disconnected from the schools. Often, retirees who see little value in being taxed for a service they no longer need and in a time of life in which their income is finite fall into that grouping. In these cases, this population will not support the budget regardless of what final form it manifests.

Regardless of communication mechanisms, there will be not only a desire to maintain tax rates, but a desire to lower tax rates while maintaining programs. While improved efficiencies and varying deliveries of programs is a method to achieve, this it is not the only way. Falling back on our previous discussions about building trust in the community is one way in which the balance in play between programs and funding can be relayed to community members.

## CASE STUDY: IMPROVING COMMUNITY ENGAGEMENT

Economic realities have spurred many school districts to regularly and purposefully engage their communities. During times in which taxes need to increase and concurrently reductions must take place, this can be difficult for the public to understand. Additionally, traditional venues for comment would have set up an adversarial environment. The goal was to develop a plan that would demonstrate how the community could work together.

An often immediate response of a school district is to have a community-based budget task force. Many of these endeavors are quite successful. The most successful example is of a large district that, at the start of an economic downturn, began a task force to look at ways to reduce costs. The task force solicited volunteers for various committees, which were open for enrollment from any members of the community. Members from the community were selected to serve on those committees.

Over a three-month time period, the task force met to review information and present findings on the representative area. As is the case with most school districts, a significant driver was personnel costs. The best perspective was to examine personnel costs as they related to the program services they were providing. For example, special education personnel both professional and support were examined in light of the classes and needs of the representative program.

Because of the need to meet economic demands and provide appropriate programs for all students, the committee then prepared their findings with recommendations to the board of directors for final approval. Final action was then in the hands of the school board, who now had a starting point and next steps. These next steps were based upon the recommendations brought forward by the committee.

- What do you anticipate some of the roadblocks would be for the board at this point?
- What benefits could the process potentially have provided?
- How could a model such as this be implemented for a variety of issues that require stakeholder engagement?

*Chapter Ten*

# Integration of Community-based Budgeting

How do you include the community in the budgeting process? Strategically, community involvement is critical to successfully passing a budget that is representative of the values and beliefs of the community.

In the opening chapter of this book, various stages in which the community is part of a budgeting process were identified. However, what does being a part of the process define? It can be easily defined as active engagement.

Active engagement is the ability for the community to work with administrators, students, staff, and the school board in a productive goal- and objective-driven environment to successfully develop a stable and realistic financial plan. This financial plan will incorporate the needs of the community in light of the values held by the community.

A district begins to integrate the community into the process through community forums. These forums provide opportunities to discuss key issues and values. Opportunities for feedback are provided. Based on these forums, there can be follow-up and appropriate responses from requisite parties.

In addition to these meetings, however, the integration of the community is part of the entire budget process. The administration should consider the values and needs for the community to provide an appropriate education for all students. Furthermore, the idea of needing to continue to connect with the community and understand their needs, wants, and desires is a part of every school board member's, administrator's, and staff's daily interactions and effort to improve the overall understanding.

Integrating community-based budgeting is not simply including components in the budget process for community feedback. It means strategically working with and educating the entire community on schools, school funding, and mandates.

The best way to further define integration is to look at your school as an entire organization. Budgets drive the function of the organization. As policy documents, they provide the guidelines and direction for years to come. For example, the elimination of new technology for one year will impede any new implementations. If technology is put back in a following year, the plan is resumed.

Viewing the budget as a policy document is the basis for integrating budgeting into the community. Yes, there is financial and technical jargon, but the heart of the process is policy decisions and strategic planning. Hence, the budget is not a standalone process, but arguably a part of the actions and decisions of each and every day for each and every community member.

An example of this integration is seen in districts that develop a long-term strategic plan. The plan integrates critical components such as needs for all students and integration of best practices. The development, implementation, and evaluation involved community feedback and insight. When the budget is impacted as a result of this document, there should be very few surprises. Furthermore, information from this plan should be calculated in the school district's forecasting model to detail impact and allow appropriate adjustments.

In addition to the strategic planning process, district committees and task forces should be inclusive of needs that can reflect budget realities. The solution to problems and issues that schools confront very often lead to a requirement for additional funding. However, there may be other options.

An example of this is that there is a need to address student discipline on buses. An "easy" yet costly fix would be to move a recommendation forward to add a monitor to the bus. This costly move would have no guarantee of addressing the issue. Other options should be explored and reviewed. Are there avenues the administration can take such as review of bus discipline, improved training for the driver, or lastly, heightened visibility of administrators on the bus emphasizing the need for good behavior?

## BUDGET AS PART OF KEY PROCESSES

Reflecting on the role of the budget as a policy, communication, and operational document, the budget is an integral part of district processes. Not only is it important in the development, but also in responding to fiscal realities that trigger heightened exploration to reduce costs, augment revenues, and increase efficiencies.

Community participation thereby influences daily actions. Through involving the community via the budget process at the ground level, there is buy-in and awareness of changes.

For example, perhaps class size is going to be increased by one to two students per year. The fiscal implications would be represented in the budget and discussed during the budget process. The process put in place would cause less alarm and hopefully provide greater understanding and would enable the administration to have ironed out issues before implementation.

As part of the next year's budget process, the change would be analyzed for effectiveness and return on investment, thereby becoming a program evaluation that is linked to programs, goals, and objectives.

## BUILDING A FIRM FOUNDATION

Beginning a community-based budgeting process may be daunting to say the least. The inability to know where ideas and feedback will come from is a mindset change. The process is best established in stages. Stages could include initial activities with parent groups and then broader more formal involvement of the community.

It is almost natural for the community to want outstanding schools that can be offered, but the approach and views on how that is best done will run the gamut. In building the process, there needs to be the involvement of those who support the schools.

Very often supporters are close to schools. In fact, they can be staff or students. It is important to ensure staff are onboard. Proven strategies include the following:

• Involving employee group leaders
• Providing opportunities for input into the operation and performance of schools
• Understanding the impact of the budget on the education
• Being knowledgeable about basic facts

All these strategies are important for supporters to spread the word about the school district. Additionally, ample opportunities for supporters from parents will prove fruitful in attracting other supporters and those who are on the fence.

The "dismayed" are often those who are disenfranchised from the school district through lack of involvement or understanding about the roles that schools play in a greater community. At times, inviting "non-parents" to functions at the local school is a way to maintain involvement. Additionally, developing an opportunity for specific feedback in the budget process about those who are disenfranchised is another venue.

Regardless of what is done, there will be those to whom the school district is not favored nor supported. In these situations, some essential merits of communication are important to consider when working with your foundation.

In his book, *Get Along with Anyone, Anytime, Anywhere,* Sanow and Strauss raise significant points relative to the need to "stick with what clicks."[1] Effective measures, including connecting with non-verbal clues, defining needs so that the public can better respect them, and avoiding defensive statements, provide an overall summary of what you can do to turn complex and dissenting conversations into a more conducive and effective discussion. Minor adjustments made in the course of a budget year to expand communication, improve outreach, and provide timely and useful information are beneficial.

Additionally, the completion of major milestones such as the successful negotiation of a favorable staff contract or implementation of a more efficient procedure will gain credibility not only with the public but also with constituents. As this momentum builds, the foundation becomes more and more solid.

As your foundation grows, the obstacles become more realistic not only due to the barriers that are broken down, but also the knowledge that the administration has relative to what will happen in a certain situation. For example, the values of the community will become prevalent. Additionally, the "untouchables or essentials" to your particular community will being to lay the course for the areas in which you are able to work to reduce expenditures and modify program to reflect the economic climate.

## CASE STUDY: BUDGET AS A STANDALONE PROCESS

A school district went through what, for the district, was a normal budget process. Information was collected and compiled, estimates were made, and a presentation on the preliminary budget was made to the board. In developing the budget, there was a need to reduce costs, which due to the amount had to be in personnel.

With the presentation of the final budget, the district transparently disclosed personnel reductions through attrition. This caused frustration in the community that the budget deficit and the resignations received dictated what the reductions would be for the next fiscal year. There appeared to be no plan as to meet educational goals, but rather a plan only to close a budget deficit.

The position of the administration and board was that these reductions prevented any furloughs or other reduction in force as the savings were achieved without disruption to staff. The public perceived that these changes would be disruptive to the program and that needs had not been considered. To counter this perception, the administration prepared data on historical information as well as rationales to the modifications from an educational standpoint.

The rationales were solid and in some cases supported the reduction in previous years, except that the staff were not retiring in that area. The public accepted most of this data, except when it came to what were valuable programs such as reading and math. Emotion began to take over as to the impact with a loss of staff in these critical areas.

- What thoughts do you have as to how this process could be improved?
- What should have been the driver of this budget and yet also would have enabled a balanced budget as an outcome?
- Could groundwork have been done with the community or would there have still been a dispute about other less "sacred" reductions?

## NOTE

1. Sanow, Arnold, and Strauss, Sandra. "Stick to What Clicks." *Get along with Anyone, Anytime, Anywhere!: 8 Keys to Creating Enduring Connections with Customers, Co-workers... Even Kids!* Garden City, NY: Morgan James Pub., 2007. 158–60.

*Chapter Eleven*

# What Works and What Does Not Work?

There is true artistry that goes into making a budget work. Meeting all the needs of the users and funders is the foundation for such masterpieces.

There are a variety of users who not only utilize budgets, but also can be said to have input into the budget process. For example, though the media attempts to report on the budget process that is underway, the media by virtue of publishing information is skewing the process from the original intent of the administration.

The media is summarizing information based on the knowledge of the individual who is reporting and what pieces are viewed to be important. An additional example is parents who review the impact of a budget and latch onto the portions that impact them, negating significant sequences of events.

These two scenarios are clear illustrations of challenges in the development of the budget process. Hence, it is of more importance than you would think relative to defining what works and the path of success in developing budgets.

## WHAT DOES NOT WORK?

It is easiest to define what does not work in a school budget. As schools are a public service, community-based budgeting develops budgets with the public in mind. There are six significant environmental and strategic decisions in developing a budget that do not work. The conditions are as follows:

- Information that is not informative and sufficient
- Simply reacting to outside feedback

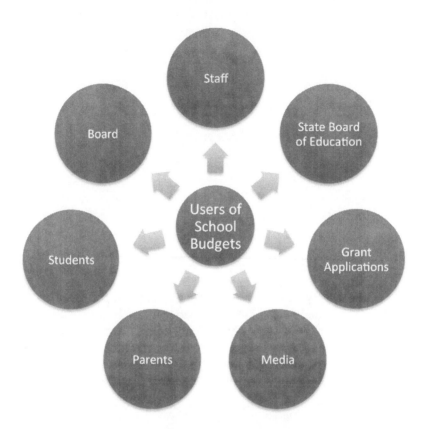

**Figure 11.1.**

- Not developing the budget with a long-term end in mind
- Inaccurate information
- Communication breakdown to internal and external constituents
- A "bully" mentality in the administration that the budget is what it is

These conditions are explained in greater detail subsequently. These conditions will never lead to successful community-based bargaining.

## INSUFFICIENT AND UNINFORMATIVE INFORMATION

Building on the discussion that there are many approaches to involving members of the community beyond just the legal requirements, this point rests on the amount of information that is made available. Certainly, there needs to be adequate information accessible to provide a proper perspective and review of the budget. For example, information should be posted on the website and be informative.

Informative can be defined as more than a one-page summary but less than the opposite end of the spectrum, which may include information that is too voluminous. Too much information will not only serve as uninformative, but as a distraction and fuel to those naysayers in your community who will use any small pieces of information against the school and advocate for their own position.

Sufficient information is that which is also informative. It is that information which will paint a picture of the story while providing details on future endeavors that are needed. Additionally, the information will need to include good solid data points and have reasonable explanation of the components. Presentations that are made to relay the progress of the budget need to be succinct yet continue to provide information and discuss the challenges and successes in the process.

There are many books and standards for budget presentations. Some of these are set at the legal level and others are an effort to provide clear communication. One of the best general formats for school districts is from the Association of School Business Officials International. This format includes summary information on the budget as a whole. Information about the organization, financial information, and a final section on additional information will lead districts to effective long-term trends.

## SIMPLY REACTING TO OUTSIDE FEEDBACK

Certainly one of the top three worst reactions an administration can have in developing the budget is to respond to what is presented in any stage relative to budget feedback and seek to make the purveyor of input happy. For example, feedback that there are too many support staff in a certain department should not warrant an immediate reaction to look to reduce staff, but the feedback should be received, noted, and reviewed through normal channels.

In most cases, making even a small adjustment can be advantageous to relaying to the public that the administration has listened. Demonstrating the feedback has been implemented to some extent will build trust between the community and the administration and board.

## NOT DEVELOPING THE BUDGET WITH A LONG-TERM END IN MIND

One of the most detrimental choices a school can make is to bridge a budget with a short-term fix so that the next year can be "gotten through." In tough economic times, schools will look to cut out new technology or utilize reserve funds to balance the budget. This strategy leads to nothing but a worse situation in the future year. To illustrate this, let's look at how in a one hundred million dollar budget, this trend can significantly worsen the financial situation for years to come.

Table 11.1 displays the fact that a deficit will continue to grow and grow when not structurally addressed. This is one of the most detrimental situations when the administration and governing board allow this to be the case and to be resolved with a one-time solution. The deficit is still there, only heightened for the subsequent year. Additionally, the challenge is only doubled for each year the trend continues, demonstrating how quickly a situation can go from bad to worse.

## INACCURATE INFORMATION

The accuracy of a budget is a reflection of the business manager, who should be able to provide succinct, accurate, and understandable information. We previously discussed the variety of formats and a preferred format for information sharing. Even without going to this measure, whatever information is shared needs to be on target with good summation as to the key points. Misleading a community even through negligence can cause havoc. For example, community members will often try to piece together information and in doing so the complete picture will not be understood. Numbers are inconsistent with previous years and unable to be explained. Inaccurate information feeds a community outcry.

## COMMUNICATION BREAKDOWN TO INTERNAL AND EXTERNAL CONSTITUENTS

While each step of the budget process needs to be properly documented, there also needs to be significant attempts to communicate. With a breakdown in communication, which can include a lack of updates, no clarification of where the process is, no information on next steps, and poor materials

**Table 11.1.**

|                   | Year 1     | Year 2      | Year 3      |
|-------------------|------------|-------------|-------------|
| **Revenues**      | 99,000,000 | 99,000,000  | 99,000,000  |
| **Expenditures**  | 98,000,000 | 100,000,000 | 101,000,000 |
| **Gap**           | 1,000,000  | (1,000,000) | (2,000,000) |
| **One-time solution** | —      | 1,000,000   | 2,000,000   |

to explain impacts to various levels of the community, there will not be a true community-based budgeting process.

While this step seems obvious, the power of communication is underestimated. Communication needs to be focused. Communication needs to have a path to reach all levels. Without a good plan, there will be a failure in reaching all constituents.

## A "BULLY" MENTALITY IN THE ADMINISTRATION

As an administrator with years of experience and significant training as to what works and what does not work, I can assure you the budget is not the place to be disrespectful to community feedback. The job of the administration is to work with the school board, and the budget is a reflection of those two levels and the community as a whole.

The budget is a plan to enable the community to fulfill what it desires its schools to be. It is not just at the time in which budgets are developed, but also throughout the process in which public involvement in our schools is critical. Some examples of these processes include strategic planning, curriculum and program development, facilities initiatives, and many additional components that make our schools strong.

## WRAPPING UP: WHAT DOES NOT WORK

Each of the factors that does not work is a significant deficiency in administering community-based budgeting. The trend amongst all points of what does not work is that each factor takes no account for the delicate balance between working with the community and bridging their vision with that of the administration. While the community vision involves passion and understanding of children, that of the administration provides insight and a platform of research to provide an appropriate education for all.

It is the role of the board to provide visioning to meet both needs. It is an important role that boards need to continue to work with as a primary purpose. School boards must have a focused vision that is communicated well to the community and held to as a guiding factor in the development of additional or reduced spending.

## WHAT DOES WORK?

Keeping the point in mind that boards need to set a vision and provide governance to the administration is important. What does work is rooted in that concept. A great board can support, nurture, guide, and build a great school system.

A poor board can tarnish, polarize, diminish the knowledge base, and decline any positive momentum. "Good" boards provide a catalyst for the other steps that are successful in community-based budgeting. These steps are more hallmarks of the process. While certainly, the steps may not be followed to the "t," they exhibit a clear sense of what community-based budgeting entails and why it is successful.

The eight hallmarks of community-based budgeting are as follows:

- Inclusion of anyone who wants to be part of the process
- Structured feedback
- Opportunities for feedback on any topic, provided in a method that is not detrimental to the larger picture
- Overviews to constituents about the budget at hand and the process
- Outside perspective
- Documentation and communication
- Honest yet substantiated responses
- Vision with the end in sight

## INCLUSION OF ANYONE WHO WANTS TO BE PART OF THE PROCESS

Perhaps in an ideal world, a limited and representative group could be chosen to provide community input. In actuality, this is the case of an elected school board and becomes the function of a representative group of community input. The purpose of community-based budgeting is to enable the entire community to come together on a matter to provide feedback and be solicited for other areas that the administration desires input.

The idea of opening up to the entire community can be daunting. The fact is, however, that based upon the spectrum that we discussed as far as involved participants, the reality is that the group which comes together even with the best publicity attempts should be manageable. The structure in other sections of what works will be even more important in working with the variety of opinions, views, and backgrounds that the group represents in your community.

## STRUCTURED FEEDBACK

Structured feedback can best be explained by reviewing what an example of unstructured feedback is. Unstructured feedback is putting up a podium and microphone for anyone who wants to come and provide comments. Such an attempt is unstructured. Anything can and more often will happen.

Furthermore, unstructured feedback will enable individuals to rattle off opinions or views from all angles. These individuals may not have even been opposed to a certain issue but because it will represent an opposition or view that is on the track with their individual views, will create a "mob" mentality.

In structured feedback, the community group is broken into smaller sub-sets. These can be by area or be homogenous in their design. The feedback needed can be presented in a topic or question form for the group to discuss and record. Following each interval of structured feedback, comments should be reported out to the larger masses. Themes will begin to develop and similar ideas can be presented in groups.

While it is not essential, these groups are created with intent or no intent as to the final composition and representation. However, always have a member of the administration and/or board of school directors as part of the group to help facilitate the process.

In the event that members of the community feel the structured questions do not allow them to provide their "original input," a space should be provided even within the group or for the entire gathering as a mechanism for any thoughts on any topic to be provided. This can be done by having committee members write or use note cards. More often than not, extreme ideas will not be that of the consensual group.

## FEEDBACK IN A DIGITAL AGE

In an age of texting, Twitter, and Facebook, schools have to embrace and utilize this technology to respond to constituents and in particular to push information out to the public.

A significant way in which the rumors or other misinformation can be corrected is through clarifying via web or other quick updates online. Following community events, communication can also be posted online to provide information on the event.

## OPPORTUNITIES FOR FEEDBACK ON ANY TOPIC

Even under the best attempts to delineate what the purpose is of your budget, there will be groups fueled by singular issues that will want to be heard. Additionally, there will be those dissidents who will utilize this as an opportunity to voice their dissenting views regardless of the community focus. Opportunities for such feedback should be provided; however, there are some quantifiers to designing this process.

The considerations in designing this process need to be such that feedback is permitted, but that it remains just that. For example, public comments that may be made from the community level may be negative and without validation. In these cases, the comments need to be permitted to be made, but not entertained if there is no merit or rationale.

One of the best methods in designing community feedback with this perspective is to utilize a large notepad with an area for feedback relative to any ideas or comments. The administration and board of directors can make their comments in writing on the board or address the feedback at a later date. This procedure minimizes the negativity that can permeate a room and the "mob mentality" which can infiltrate and change the dynamics.

## OVERVIEWS TO CONSTITUENTS ABOUT THE BUDGET AT HAND AND THE PROCESS

A framework has to be presented from the beginning of the budget process. This framework needs to be reiterated at each and every opportunity to frame the issues at hand and what is at work and factors for consideration within the development of the budget.

Building a budget is not directly about deciding to eliminate all non–school-based administrators or looking to close the school district and go charter. The issue at hand is the budget before you with the assumptions and turn of events put into perspective for brainstorming, troubleshooting, and feedback. While it may be true that reducing administrators may save money, it has to be as part of a broader plan.

Focus is the key word to remember during the budget process. Input must be related to the issues at hand. The budget can and often will become a catalyst for solving issues and concerns. Going back to the premise that the budget must be a consideration in all community engagement opportunities is key to the process. The work during the preparation and review of a final annual budget must be related to that and not drawing in outside issues.

## OUTSIDE PERSPECTIVE

In both prosperous and difficult times, each and every community-based budgeting process must work within trends and policy decisions of education and at the national, state, and local levels. Economic and other political and social changes can drastically impact what an administration and board of directors are able to accomplish.

Maintaining community awareness of many issues is a fundamental part of the budget process. Decisions cannot be made without proper perspectives.

Additionally, communities are all too quick to lose sight of factors beyond the board's and administrators' control. This is important in building a consensus about what steps to take and what actions to move on or delay.

## DOCUMENTATION AND COMMUNICATION

Documentation of both the process and budget construction to a final document is important to build confidence from budget stakeholders in the process as well as to record initiatives, actions, public statements, and solidify community input. Exceeding legal requirements, but not needing to be highly sophisticated, is what works best in the process.

While not needing to be sophisticated, the information needs to be electronic in presence, easily accessible, and understandable from a lay perspective. Information should not just be in the common PowerPoint format, but with background and perhaps guided narration or summary statements to allow the true message to come through. Information *must* be communicated consistently.

## HONEST YET SUBSTANTIATED RESPONSES

Rightfully so, there is an ever pressing push for transparency in our education system. The biggest way to enable this while avoiding an information overload is to substantiate responses to the community. Responses need to include specific details on the steps that will be taken and on the impact. As previously discussed, vague responses will only serve to incite the community.

## VISION FOR THE END IN SIGHT

The process and involvement of the community needs to have a direction. Additionally, there needs to be a path set for the end in sight relative to the process. Discussions can and will continue. Providing answers to questions, resolute responses and direction, and a structured process, the conclusion of community involvement will enhance, support, and establish a final document. This final document will represent the values and direction for the school district both short- and long-term.

## PERSPECTIVE OF A COMMUNITY

It is rather easy to apply a budgeting program in an academic sense. Our discussion to this point has focused on the importance of a variety of factors and steps in a "community-based budgeting process."

To truly understand the process, it is valuable to look at the application of steps and methods on three school districts with varying situations, circumstances, wealth, and other factors. Through the eyes of these three districts, we can see that there is an ability to implement the process outlined regard-

less of circumstances provided certain adaptations are made that do not significantly deviate the process from its truest intent.

The first lens of application is with an urban school district. This district
would be focused on improving student achievement in an economically
disadvantaged population. For example, the school district is seeking to make
grounds in core academics while dealing with concerns with state and local
revenue sources. The public is rather disconnected from the schools, and
there is little interest for additional involvement except from the board and a
few active citizen groups.

Perhaps the most difficult implementation obstacle in this case is the lack
of involvement. Regardless of how many community meetings are coordinated, attendance will be light with the core attendees being those most informed in the process. The real counter to this obstacle is the need to attract
core collaboration from the community based upon targeting groups for involvement.

Community service groups such as the Lions or Rotary are great outlets
for involvement. Additionally, the significant need for social services in such
a community indicates the need to include those functions in the process.
What can be gained from this targeted involvement is not only input but also
support for the broader goals and priorities at hand.

In a community such as this, raising taxes is the easy way out of an
economic situation. More money does not necessarily equate to higher performing schools. More money will not make the schools a true representation
of their community. Lack of money in the right programs and opportunities,
on the other hand, will present a roadblock.

It is critical to express to the community the need for supportive direction.
The involvement and support is what will in part enable the district to tra-
verse a tumultuous economic situation.

Another implementation scenario is a suburban school district that is a
certain distance from a major metropolitan area. Under this scenario, there
will be a plethora of involved community members who value the school
system and its role in the community. Parents and other community members
routinely deliberate on the balance between paying more revenues and the
value of maintaining, expanding or reducing existing programs.

In this situation, the community is best served under a budget model that
incorporates budget into day-to-day cycles. For example, in the adoption of a
textbook cycle, an ongoing cycle that allows the entire curriculum to be at
one state or another is beneficial so that the program evolves and comes in
and out of the budget. Decisions can me made on a multiyear basis regarding
whether to move forward or to pause in the cycle. Additionally, comprehensive approaches to incorporating best practices can allow adjustments from
year to year-based on fiscal constraints. For example in one year, if funds

cannot be allocated for an initiative, preparations and prioritization for future years can be made.

In a third lens, a budget for a rural school districts perhaps face some of the most unique challenges covering large or small geographic areas. In a scenario with a rural school district, here is not only a reduced efficiency very often due to geography, but also due to economics. In certain cases, rural economic factors for income can lead to substantial changes in annual local revenues. Additionally, exemptions real estate taxes which are very often a primary source of revenue for schools, provide additional revenue challenges. Building on the suburban school, the ability to have a multi-year plan is beneficial. Additionally, improvements to reduce operational costs are beneficial to direct funds to classroom instruction.

Regardless of the situation, understanding the community is the basis for a successful outcome. Budgets are not a one size fits all approach, however, the ability to adapt best practices to the matter at hand can be a key tool for successful outcomes. Finally, the value of local benchmarking and regional comparative data is of the utmost importance in guiding the budget process and ensuring a good outcome.

*Chapter Twelve*

# Resiliency

One of the best ways a district can continue its momentum is to develop an end in sight and stick to plotting a path to the desired result. Perhaps easier said than done, it can be a focus to enable momentum when there are factions opposed to a specific action.

One of the best ways to maintain resiliency is to respond with "tactics" to address needs with the appropriate person. Recall from Chapter 2 that there are those who are internal to your organization and those who are external. Additionally, within the internal and external groupings, there are those who are in one of the six stages of involvement ranging from synergistic to irrational.

## INTERNAL CHALLENGES

One of the largest challenges in fact can come from internal misperceptions. For example, the staff in the day-to-day environment often believe that they have knowledge of how to make a budget work. The common perception is that there is plenty of money and that it is just a matter of priorities.

One way to work to eliminate an internal belief that there is a misperception about budget funding sources is to demonstrate how budgets are allocated. In particular, the various restrictions that grants and other restrictive funding may provide. Additionally, the ability to link the budget back to the values of the community discussed in Chapter 1 is important to note. Those values that often include increasing student learning are priorities on an annual basis.

There must be a true strategy to how this information is relayed to the community. A starting point is a presentation of information to administrators, including central- and building-based information, to enable them to share the information as an update with their respective areas. Information that is shared out by the respective building or area staff provides the opportunity for staff with specific questions.

Once information is shared with staff, there should be follow-up on the process and other important information. The goal is to continue a cycle of trust and appropriate disclosure.

## EXTERNAL CHALLENGES

From an external perspective, parents, community leaders, and those community members with no vested interest to the schools such as retirees create the composition of external factors to be resilient to.

More often than not, parents will support or dissent on factors that impact their child. For example, the modification to a gifted program that will reduce operating costs. Another example is reducing class size at the elementary school level.

Communicating with a group that is external yet involved with the school is one of the most difficult aspects of working with a community. There is a significant amount of emotion and loss of focus on facts at this point in the process. As was said before, holding true to the end in sight is the best strategy.

To reinforce certain points and to communicate with parents, leaders of the parent groups should be resources for the administration. These individuals can empathize with individual personalities and personal issues.

It is important that the focus to these individuals be immediate and not only provide information, but permit a response to the administration with feedback. The school district should also provide sample printed information for distribution for those publications, blogs, and other web media that it utilized to distribute to those unable to attend the face to face meeting.

In striving to work through the roadblocks, ordinary mediums such as quarterly newsletters, mid-year updates, and goal meeting presentations should incorporate key ideas regarding the budget. Identifying a focus to show that changes can work within existing goals would be a positive outcome as well.

For example, the district's strategic plan that ordinarily covers a five- to seven-year period should include information on impact of the budget as well as demonstrate that despite budget limitations, goals can be achieved and steps can be taken in the process.

In addition to external parents, there are also those who have no children in the schools. These individuals or families may not be aware of the opportunities the district provides and of the obstacles the district faces as it works through economic realities. In fact, very often these individuals remain neutral and are a great source to utilize for support. In seeking to come back from a hard knock or disconcertion regarding a program reduction, these individuals can serve as a resource.

Many districts reach those external individuals through a newsletter, which is a good ongoing way to provide positive information. Additionally, in response to criticism, it may be valuable to hold specific sessions with these individuals to discuss their input into the process.

A final group of external critics is the media. While providing them information that is handy for their culmination of information is a good step, meetings with media can also be a valuable resource. Unfortunately, emotion plays into the stories and that often skews the portrayal. The facts, however, should be indisputable and provide information that emotion cannot be attached to.

An example of this is a district that looked to reduce aides. While there was data to support the cause, the administration developed a linear plan that provided useful information as to how the reduction of aides would improve access. Full-time aides were being reduced, but part-time replacements were being put in place. The district would save the medical expenditures as well as some salary, but the sell to the community was greater flexibility.

The school district told the story how they would be able to utilize part-timers to meet various immediate needs such as parents not picking up on time or to cover event days when there was a need for more adult presence. With this spin, there was a positive counter to the fact that there was a loss of full-time support.

## HOW TO MOTIVATE OTHERS

As budgets consume significant time and energy for the board, community, and administration, stakeholders can lose energy. Motivation from leadership is key to continuing the process. Often, reflection on the steps to date and the progress made can serve not only as positive reinforcement, but can trigger thoughts of how previous obstacles were resolved.

The role of motivation can land with either an administrator or board member, but most often is in the hands of the superintendent. Relating to the experiences and reinforcing the workload accomplished to date can be one method for motivation. Additionally, posing solutions and focusing on the important components can focus the budget process on concrete and achievable objectives.

An additional motivational factor is continued empowerment to those revising and responding to community feedback. Successful budget development comes from empowered individuals collaborating to achieve a common goal, yet meeting the needs, wants, and desires of their department or building. To achieve a successful end product as revisions are made to a budget in response to structured feedback, empowerment must continue through the conclusion of the budget development process.

## DEALING WITH DIFFICULT CONSTITUENCIES

Dealing with difficult personalities is perhaps the most challenging obstacle to maintain motivation. Often a few personalities emerge to the forefront on not simply an original point of discontent but also other issues. For example, an individual who disagrees with a tax hike may then move to overall dissatisfaction with other unrelated factors.

Some methodologies for working with difficult personalities will be discussed later in this chapter. However, no strategy will be effective without listening. Listening is one of the most critical steps to resolve disagreement. Listening will not solve the entire issue, but it is necessary for the following reasons:

- Listening will allow the other side to consider the core issue.
- Listening provides the opportunity to express that there can be a resolution.
- As schools draw from public funds, listening is a requirement due to the critical component of stewardship.

Once the act of "listening" has occurred, there can be a clarification by the other party. For example, clarifications are best to provide information on the facts and to clarify misconceptions. Additionally, there may be the opportunity to come to agreement, but often that will not be accomplished.

When faced with a lack of agreement, there should be flexibility to acknowledge valid and substantiated points with steps that demonstrate receptiveness and changes based upon the feedback. A case study will best demonstrate this critical balance, which provides an adjustment based upon listening, but does not change position or entire direction of the initiative.

## CASE STUDY: A REDUCTION PROCESS

When working through the annual budget in which revenues reflected a national economic crisis paired with a political desire to reduce school funding while providing resources for school choice, a district was faced with a deficit of over five million dollars. The deficit was not one that could be filled through tax increases, so there would need to be expenditures reductions.

In considering options, the administration presented a list of reductions. These reductions included staff, resources, and improved efficiencies that were required to balance the budget. Information was presented to the community soliciting feedback relative to the budget. In particular, considerations were made for benchmark data that were available and comparable. Data showed high staffing in certain areas.

In light of the data, the political scene was such that the community perceived that the positions were necessary and the district was an anomaly relative to its needs disposition. Letters and emails flooded the board and administration on certain positions. Editorials and blogs criticized the proposed measures. However, there was no recognition that maintenance of "outlier" positions would only increase budgetary constraints.

Throughout the process, the administration and board listened to the community. The involvement peaked when not only certain positions came to question, but also other matters relative to the budget. While the administration viewed that all the proposed reductions were necessary, there was an ability to modify the largest positions that were challenged by the community, but maintain the balance.

This demonstration of listening and providing information relative to concerns addressed was not folding as the majority of the reductions were maintained. The ability of the administration and board to listen and demonstrate why the remainder of the reductions had to be maintained.

The community was proud and in turn acknowledged the difficult steps that had to be taken during these challenging times.

## TACTICS FOR WORKING WITH DIFFICULT PERSONALITIES

Perhaps tactics is misleading and methods is more appropriate, but as a seasoned administrator, I can say that working with difficult personalities is truly tactical. There must be an identification relative to the issues at hand and desired outcomes. As discussed previously, there can be a variety of perspectives that comes to the forefront and dissents with the consensus.

## RESILIENCY

Resiliency is perhaps a critical component to ensuring a process reaches its success. There will be numerous times in which the budget work group might feel they have hit the end, but there has to be a moment for reflection and a strong desire to strive to achieve the end that is in sight.

Always remember, in light of the challenges presented, there will be an end in sight. Challenges will be both internal and external with perhaps the internal challenges proving the most difficult to accomplish. These two categories of challenges are listed in Table 12.1.

Often, roadblocks will include working with community groups that are singular in nature and concerns. Often, it is advantageous to work from the end goal backwards.

For example, if an issue is a reduction in support staff for instructional purposes, look to the end goal, which is reduced expenditures and similar program components. Work with this group to explain how the requisite requirements will be met. For example, needs can be met through more efficient means such as through assistive technology.

Resiliency is also important in moving forward. From an internal and external perspective, it is critical in working to continue to do more with less to improve the educational experience for students.

Throughout the course of a budget process, you form connections and understandings that individuals or special interest groups may bring to the table. It is important that as part of process the various perspectives do not derail the budget from the primary purpose, which is to provide programs to all students. Additionally, the ability to respond to concerns from a variety of interests is key to enabling the budget process to continue to move to final budget adoption.

**Table 12.1.**

| Internal Challenges | External Challenges |
| --- | --- |
| Morale | Countering external efforts |
| Working through misconceptions | Providing detail yet not responding to nuances |
| Aligning wants and desires to resources available | Maintaining engagement and understanding of stakeholders |

*Chapter Thirteen*

# Celebrate Success

Success can be at times hard to find. A process never moves smoothly. As was previously shown, there are always deviations. It is important to as a team of community, staff, and board members to work together and jointly celebrate success.

## DOCUMENT!

Documenting successful measures affords an opportunity to provide evidence of accomplishments. Positive news in light of the negative that often is associated with the budget process due to reductions or increased taxation will increase trust and demonstrate the need to serve multiple perspectives. A milestone such as successful negotiations or implementing a long-range fix to an obstacle is a tribute to the community, board, and administration working together for results.

Utilizing the media for publicizing success is paramount. Additionally, locally produced media such as through social media, a website, and You-tube are great venues to put the word out and to demonstrate the success of the process. Finally, recognition and sharing with colleagues in neighboring schools provides the ability for replication and solidification of the district's process.

## PUBLICIZE YOUR SUCCESS

The news media is usually eager to publish adverse information about schools ordinarily fueled by tips from those disgruntled with either higher taxes and/or a loss of programs. When a school works with their community to reach a desired outcome, it is also important for the school district to seek appropriate media outlets for its information.

Schools that are involving the community in their budget process should invite the media to attend their public meetings and provide summaries of the process and impacts to reporters. The more knowledgeable reporters are about the way a school budget works, the more accurate depictions they will make for both school and public triggered media needs.

It is perhaps elementary to simply make the statement to utilize the media. The school district needs to have a media list and engage media to include online blogs and other sources the community utilizes for information on a particular topic.

Before the core budget process and community involvement begins, there should be tremendous outreach to showcase accomplishments and other "stand out" indicators. For example:

- Does the school offer more advanced placement courses than others in a particular region or state?
- What colleges have graduates gone onto?
- What alumni have reached a pinnacle in their career?
- What merits have been determined through data benchmarking of areas in which the district excels?

Celebrating success can also mean demonstrating resources that are going toward student achievement. Inviting the media and the community into school buildings can send an extremely positive message about the school and what is happening within the buildings.

## THE PROCESS OF IMPLEMENTING THE BUDGET

The process of budget implementation is as detailed and involved as the development. Many of the steps are guided by administrative steps to comply and meet mandates. Implementation is not without the option for public feedback.

On a monthly or quarterly basis, financials are presented. Very often due to unforeseen circumstances or changes in trends, budget information is up-dated and often adapted. Budget implementation incorporates the policy and organizational components previously discussed.

## ACCOUNTING

With the approval of a final budget, the administration begins to prepare purchases. This involves updating preliminary quotes and staffing estimates with actual expenditures. Through this step, expenditures may be higher or lower than budgeted.

In many cases, when expenditures exceed estimates, there is a need to review other areas for expenditures that may be less than expected or as a final solution to determine what expenditures will not occur. In certain cases, the expenditures may be able to be funded through a reserve category or revenue projections that exceed estimates.

Board or state policy will dictate how significant budget changes must be communicated to the public. In the absence of a requirement to communicate, it is a best practice that changes of significance be regularly reported to the board of directors for approval. Additionally, while the budget is implemented, there can be updates to the community.

An easy method to update the community is through the development of an easy-to-read dashboard. Providing charts and graphs can easily allow anyone to view performance. Additionally, presentations can be made to stand-alone or as part of the budget process for the next year to benchmark performance as well as whether revenues and expenditures have performed better or worse than expected.

## YEAR-END FISCAL PERFORMANCE

Most school districts prepare a year-end accounting report. This can be via an annual financial report or a year-end audit. As part of community-based budgeting, the communication of financial performance is essential not only for transparency but also as part of a continuous channel of communication between the district and all constituents.

## CASE STUDY: CELEBRATE SUCCESS

In tough economic times, there is usually little cause for celebration; however, school districts have had the ability to celebrate. One district celebrated innovative ideas to provide budget relief. The annual event brought community, staff, and board members together.

For the event, a story board approach was used and individuals with ideas for reductions highlighted their ideas and how those ideas would implement cost savings. Community members and other attendees were able to peruse the room similar to a science fair format to obtain information on the reductions. It was always a well-attended and informative event.

Perhaps even more so than providing ideas for cost reductions, the event provided a venue for open a non-confrontational dialogue. Additionally, there was the involvement and attendance of those who ordinarily would not attend a normal meeting to discuss the budget. The celebration provided many ideas, but perhaps the benefits were more than simply the ideas for cost savings.

- What opportunities can you identify to celebrate success?
- In thinking of opportunities, there would also be the ability to engage a wider audience. What benefits would this provide?

*Chapter Fourteen*

# Takeaway

When a community works collaboratively to improve schools, the children, community, and greater societal impact of education are improved. It is my hope that this publication provides not only a sense of urgency, but also a firm basis for parents, retirees, singletons, and others both vested and un-vested in education to support local programs.

There are some great ways in which community involvement can take place. To start, for those with children matriculating in the schools, there are parent and other advocacy groups. Additionally, elected school board members and appointed administrators are more than willing to hear constructive feedback and obtain solid substantiated feedback.

If you are not connected to the school program, there are opportunities at public meetings and other events which benefit the school program to take part and support education. Working with parent and other advocacy organizations is also a way in which to champion the causes and direction that is being expressed.

While a school district exists to represent an entire community, difficult economics or other factors will require difficult decisions at one point or another. For example, even the most affluent district may face a political reduction in state funding. On the other hand, an impoverished district may need to modify delivery of services to meet the needs of all students and the need to reduce expenditures.

School boards and administrators welcome feedback from constituents. Often, the feedback is at odds with the direction that needs to take place. It is ultimately the role of the board of directors and administration to take all the feedback and consider the values of the community in light of the obstacles, challenges, and needs of all students.

Community members will sometimes respond with "the community was not heard" to the fact that decisions contrary to their group's opinion go into effect despite vocal opposition. An example of this is the often unfavorable reductions that take place as a result of economics. While a decision or action may move forward, the concerns that have been raised are usually considered in light of taking the action.

For example, the fact raised by the community that a reduction of building support staff may lead to greater discipline issues. The decision to reduce support staff may have to be made in light of benchmarking and other cost containment procedures. It is, however, the job of the administration and board to consider the points raised and to ensure that despite the necessity for the action to take place, the concerns of the community will be addressed. This can be done through annual updates and informational activities for the community.

Addressing concerns means ensuring the appropriate mechanisms are put in place to accommodate the ongoing needs. The budget reality in schools, businesses, and non-profits is to do more with less. Districts must relay to the community steps that will be taken to address the concerns.

Often, a response to address concerns will not suffice. A great strategy or way to truly demonstrate the fact that concerns or issues raised in light of reductions will be addressed is to have scenarios or case studies on the facts. These real and factual examples can often concisely and appropriately address concerns and how the administration will react. The involvement of the community and appropriate personnel involved in the issue at hand is of critical importance as the school district works to address concerns.

## CASE STUDY CONCLUSIONS

The case studies that were presented at various intervals in this book were demonstrative of the ability to work through issues and come up with solutions. Each study was not presented with an absolute answer or outcome until this point.

Weaving the studies together, they demonstrate the impact that communities can have through working with situations for the best result. The solutions in all cases of the studies can be summarized into three successful steps. These steps include active listening, responsiveness, and progressing along a path that is avoids being absolute and unresponsive to the community, but also avoids not changing direction and course simply because of dissent.

### Active Listening

Active listening is often a forgotten tactic. Becoming defensive of a position is often a more immediate response than to actively listen. In the early 1980s, the American communication researchers, Steil, Watson, and Barker, developed the SIER hierarchy of active listening based on their observation that people recall only about 50 percent of the message immediately after hearing it and only 25 percent after two days. Steil, Watson, and Barker built upon Claude Shannon and Warren Weaver's general model of communication that was first published in 1947. Active listening—necessary to fully internalizing verbal and non-verbal messages of buyers—is a skill that helps salespeople be more effective in the sales process.

The SIER model is a hierarchical, four-step sequence of listening activities:

1. Sensing: The hierarchy of active listening begins by hearing, seeing, and receiving the verbal and non-verbal aspects of the message. Concentration is required in this phase. The buyer should not be interrupted so the message can be delivered in full and with adequate detail. The receiver's body language should be positive to help the sender deliver the message.

2. Interpreting: After receiving the message, the salesperson must interpret and place it in meaningful context. The buyer's experiences, knowledge, and attitudes should be linked to the verbal and non-verbal elements of the message. Interpreting helps insure that the receiver's understanding corresponds to the sender's meaning.

3. Evaluating: Active listening occurs at the evaluation phase after the interpretation phase. The receiver must sort fact from opinion. The receiver needs to judge the message based on its strengths and weaknesses, and how well it is liked or disliked. The evaluation phase consists of both logical and emotional components.

4. Responding: Two-way communication requires the receiver to respond to the sender. The response provides feedback to the sender on how well the message was understood and encourages further interaction between the two parties. Responses can be both verbal and non-verbal. Rephrasing and reflecting the sender's message shows interest and increases understanding. Pruning questions provides additional detail and clarification.[1]

Active listening was one of the most common themes in the case studies. It is a critical skill for school board members and administrators to utilize in working through community-based budgeting. The ability to listen to stakeholders and encourage feedback is a successful tactic.

The case study with the administration evaluating three budget options required the administration to actively listen to not only each other, but their community not necessarily at the time of the decision, but in the course of their involvement with the community. The decision of which option to select rests with the administration's ability to determine not only the best solution, but one that will garner the most support and is a reflection of the community's values.

In the situation of community conversations, the administration listened to any issues that surfaced. While issues were not necessarily resolved nor did the community conversations yield any significant outcome, they enabled the administration to listen to an audience pulled together on a matter.

In this same manner, the development of district task forces is a critical direction of active listening. Whether the task forces yield the desired outcome is dependent upon responsiveness and the ability to maintain a direction; in each task force case, they provided an opportunity for active listening.

## Responsiveness

Though active listening in part involves responding, responsiveness means demonstrating to the public that insight, feedback, and suggestions have been considered and to some extent incorporated into the project. A great tactic in demonstrating responsiveness is to give in to one thing and hold firm on the remainder. For example, understanding the situation of the poor school district, the ability to provide responsive action to a situation speaks volumes to a community. Whether the outcome is completed in full may depend upon the district's fiscal situation, but the responsiveness is key to effective community relations.

Additionally, utilizing the budget as a means of responsiveness incorporates several realities seen in the case studies. The budget as a policy document recognizes the district's response to either policy concerns or to modify program delivery. Additionally, decisions on including a cyber model of education means making a policy decision due to the fiscal implications, which is considered in the course of budget development.

The reality is that the budget cannot be a standalone document. The budget must be considered to be responsive to community needs, wants, and desires. Any attempt otherwise alienates the core mission of school districts, which is to deliver educational programs.

## Maintaining Direction

Arguably, maintaining direction, though sensible in theory, is a challenge to deliver. The forces both internal and external as part of the delivery can cause delay. For example, in the development of task forces, there will be a multitude of ideas that branch off of the trunk or core issue at hand. The key is to maintain focus, yet provide an opportunity for individuals to be heard, yet for the task force to deliver a product that attains the desired outcome.

Additionally, the provision of electronic budgets, which include a dashboard of information, is a way a district maintains direction with a current form of information delivery. The ability for additional access can increase the available information, but also provide too much information or information sharing that is not necessarily along the main route at hand.

The decision to outsource is significant. Turning over valued staff to an outside vendor is a difficult decision. Before going in this direction, the district should consider what the road entails. There will undoubtedly be community dissent and other adverse situations. If the decision is still to proceed, then the task should be completed.

A situation as complex as outsourcing involves many milestones that require continued approval. The reality is approval should not be rubber stamped, but also not shied away from due to unpleasant reactions. This is easier said than done, but it is critical to a successful decision at the end of the process.

A component of maintaining direction is to make consistent and adequate progress at each review or step. Simply "spinning wheels" around and around without movement to the next level stalls the process. This also can show uncertainty or provide too much of a focus on a particular step on the road to completion.

## FINAL THOUGHTS

This book has sought to provide insight and practical methods and scenarios to readers. The next step in community-based budgeting is to become involved in your school district's budget process and actively participate in the process. Regardless of whether the approach is executed with exactitude, the process and end result will reflect the norms of the community served.

As no two community-based budget processes will look alike, there will of course be certain similarities. These similarities include engagement, strategic decision-making for all students, and an appropriate allocation of finite resources that can respond to an ever changing environment.

## NOTE

1. Lyman K. Steil, Larry L. Barker and Kittie W. Watson. Effective listening Key to your success. Addison-Wesley. United States 1983. http://www.provenmodels.com/554/sier-hierarchy-of-active-listening/kittie-w.-watson--larry-l.-barker--lyman-k.-steil/ Accessed March 31, 2014.

CPSIA information can be obtained at www.ICGtesting.com
Printed in the USA
BVOW05s0249160514

353662BV00001B/3/P